THE
LOUISIANA
SEAFOOD
BIBLE

THE
LOUISIANA
SEAFOOD
BIBLE

Oysters

Jerald and Glenda Horst

PELICAN PUBLISHING COMPANY
Gretna 2011

The word "Pelican" and the depiction of a pelican are
trademarks of Pelican Publishing Company, Inc., and are
registered in the U.S. Patent and Trademark Office.

Library of Congress Cataloging-in-Publication Data

Horst, Jerald.
  The Louisiana seafood bible : oysters / by Jerald And Glenda Horst.
      p. cm.
  Includes index.
  ISBN 978-1-58980-969-7 (hardcover : alk. paper) 1. Cooking (Oysters)
2. Cooking, American--Louisiana style. 3. Oysters--Louisiana. 4. Oyster
industry--Louisiana. 5. Cookbooks. I. Horst, Glenda. II. Title. III. Title:
Oysters.

  TX754.O98.H67 2011
  641.6'94--dc22

                                        2011010722

Front jacket photograph by Daniel Leyten.

Printed in China

Published by Pelican Publishing Company, Inc.
1000 Burmaster Street, Gretna, Louisiana 70053

Twas a brave man indeed that 'et the first oyster.

Jonathan Swift (1667-1745),
Irish poet, political writer, and clergyman

You needn't tell me that a man who doesn't love oysters and asparagus and good wines has got a soul, or a stomach either. He simply has an instinct for being unhappy.

Hector Hugh Monro (1870-1916),
Scottish-born British writer who wrote under the pen name "Saki"

As I ate the oysters with their strong taste of the sea and their faint metallic taste that the cold wine washed away, leaving only the sea taste and the succulent texture, and as I drank their cold liquid from each shell and washed it down with the crisp taste of the wine, I lost the empty feeling and began to be happy and make plans.

Ernest Hemingway (1899-1961),
American novelist and journalist

Contents

Preface

This is volume four of the *Louisiana Seafood Bible*. Preceding volumes were dedicated to shrimp, crawfish, and crabs. The information in this book, as in its three predecessors, is the result of Glenda and my experiences inside the industry. Glenda grew up the daughter of a commercial fisherman, living in a tiny commercial fishing community. I spent thirty years as a Sea Grant marine advisory agent and LSU Agricultural Center professor of fisheries.

One of my missions was to develop and transfer to the fishing industry better methods of harvesting, processing, and marketing the bounty of Louisiana's waters. Being involved from the sea to the table, I received an education about the inner workings of this fascinating business that few outside the industry are privileged to ever see.

During the course of my career, I published a monthly fisheries newsletter called *Lagniappe*. Each edition ended with a recipe. Many of the recipes in this book were originally published in that newsletter. Some of the recipes came from Glenda and my personal test kitchen, but less than 10 percent of our efforts made the cut and were printed in the newsletter.

A larger number of recipes were sent in voluntarily by the readers of the newsletter, with the understanding that they would be publically shared. Glenda and I tested each and every recipe we received. About half of them were deemed worthy of printing.

Finally, Glenda and I love to travel and eat. We have been fortunate enough to meet many others who love seafood as we do. Many of these people have worked within the seafood industry, but a surprising number were dedicated seafood lovers from all walks of life. These people have invited Glenda and me into their homes to share the experience of preparing their family heirloom recipes. These experiences have been beyond delightful and have left us with many warm memories, as well as world-class recipes.

This book is a joint effort with my wife and cooking partner, Glenda. It is written in the first person by me only for the sake of being easier to read than if the reader had to switch between the two of us constantly.

We would like to paraphrase a quote by Joan Reardon, from the description of her 2004 book *Oysters: A Culinary Celebration.* "Come into our kitchen; we would like our oysters to meet you."

Eat hearty!

Jerald Horst

Acknowledgements

A book of this type is a complex creature and would have died aborning without the willing and open help of many people. We are grateful to all of those whose help was so generously offered with no compensation. David Guilbeau, Gordon LeBlanc, Buddy Pausina, Harlon Pearce, Benjy Rayburn, Al Sunseri, and Mike Voisin answered many questions for us about oysters and the oyster industry. The Louisiana Seafood Promotion and Marketing Board helped us clear many small hurdles. We thank Bozidar Cibilic, Mitch and Frank Jurisich, and Pete Vujnovich Jr., for producing and donating superlative oysters for our recipe-testing and photographic work when oysters were difficult to find in the aftermath of the BP oil spill.

We are indebted to Capt. Pete Vujnovich Jr., Wilbert Collins, Al Sunseri, Sal Sunseri, John Tesvich, and Mike Voisin for welcoming us onto their fishing boats or into their businesses with our intrusive camera and for sharing their world with us. We also want to thank those people who donated recipes throughout the years. Thanks are extended to Mark Schexnayer for providing access to archived historical photographs and to Karen Wicker for providing a copy of her PhD dissertation, which provided valuable historical information.

Deepest thanks are extended to the following individuals who welcomed us into their homes and businesses while they prepared the recipes that they shared with us: George Barisich, Melanie Charpentier, Eva Alario Corcoran, Caryl Curtis, Tommy Cvitanovich, Carolyn Falgout, Andrea Galiano, Frank Jurisich, Mitch Jurisich Jr., Carol Keltz, Charlie Lieux, Colette and Allen Lottinger, Joe and Cheryl Macaluso, Ed McIntyre, Alex Patout, Jeff and Mary Poe, Rose and Kenneth Palombo, John and Karen Supan, Ann and Tony Taylor, John and Jane Tesvich, Dudley and Kim Vandenborre, and Eva Vujnovich.

Sincere thanks are extended to the following institutions and individuals for generously sharing, without compensation, their photographs and time for personal interviews: Enola Dazet Balliviero, George Barisich, Dominica Cibilich, Wilbert Collins, Brian Gauvin, the Iberia Parish Library, Mitch Jurisich Sr., the Jefferson Parish Yearly Review, Jean Landry, John Matranga, Ralph "Buddy" Pausina, John Tesvich, and Eva Vujnovich.

The strongest gratitude possible is reserved for Lisa Winterburn and Ginger Corkern. Both took time out from their busy schedules for re-testing recipes for this book and setting them up for photography. Cooking non-stop all day is grueling and creating original arrangements that are photographically friendly is mentally taxing. Glenda and I could not have accomplished our goals without these two valiant volunteers.

And finally, John Supan! This book would never have come together without him. He was our rock of advice, transporter of oysters for photo shoots and test cooking, contributor of recipes, source of everyone and anyone's contact information, and gushing fount of technical and practical advice. He never seemed to weary of our phone calls. Thank you, John.

It takes a village to create a book.

Part I: Oysters

Oyster Mania

For being such a homely creature, the oyster has captivated mankind since antiquity. The creature is simple; it has neither eyes nor legs. At first appearance it resembles nothing so much as a rough-surfaced rock, often encrusted with barnacles, strands of algae, and other marine life. After its top shell has been pried off, it is even less attractive to the eye. Naked of any lovable, appetizing, or even colorful feature, it appears formless and phlegmy. One questions whether it is a kind of independent life.

Oh, but when a salty, perfectly fat winter oyster, with no embellishments to hide its taste, is placed on the tongue! A flood of all the briny flavors of the sea cascades through your mouth. As your tongue rolls the oyster over, the body, so turgidly swollen with winter fat, breaks into creamy pieces and coats the inside of your mouth like

Sonya "Black Widow" Thomas set a world record at the 2010 Acme Oyster Eating World Championship in New Orleans.

fresh butter. A few chews and your eye teeth find the firm, but not tough, scallop-like adductor muscle that most people call the "eye." It offers just enough tooth resistance to finish the bite. After it goes down, your taste buds are left ringing with a copper tang, finished with a hint of lemon.

You want another one.

Ancient Romans certainly appreciated oysters. Author and historian, Pliny the Elder called oysters, "the palm and pleasure of the table." The wealthy and inventive Roman, Sergius Orata, reportedly introduced oyster cultivation using oysters from Bendisi to bed in Lake Lucrinus near Rome. (He also invented an early hot tub.) As early as 78 BC, Romans transported oysters in bags, tightly packed with snow and ice to the city.

In her book *Oysters: A Culinary Celebration,* (Lyons Press), culinary historian and biographer Joan Reardon notes that, "Romans consumed bushels of oysters, relishes, mushrooms, peacocks eggs, and sardines as appetizers. But oysters were so popular that they were used as an accompaniment to roasted boar and other entrées and were served throughout an entire orgy."

In 55 BC, the Romans conquered Briton and discovered vast beds of oysters growing in the Thames River estuaries. Roman historian Sallust (Gaius Sallustius Crispus) dryly observed, "Poor Britons, there is some good in them after all—they produce an oyster."

The Roman love for oysters was passed on to other Europeans after the collapse of the empire. A sixteenth century traveler to England said oysters, "which were cried in every street," were better than he had seen in Italy. Louis XIV, the great French Sun King, held oysters in particular favor. Casanova, the Venetian adventurer and

© *Hearst Corporation Service*

womanizer, is said to have eaten fifty every morning for breakfast. By the nineteenth century, oysters became increasingly available to the common man, as well as the wealthy, in all of Europe.

Meanwhile, back in the U.S., or rather what was eventually to become the United States, early colonists found quantities of oysters beyond the imagination. British colonists first tasted New World oysters in 1607, and John Smith wrote home from Virginia during the Christmas season, "we were never more merry nor fed on more plenty of good oysters." A century and a half later, George Washington also enjoyed dining on oysters.

Oyster production in the early part of the nineteenth century was focused near New York and to a lesser degree the Chesapeake Bay. New York was also the early center for the oyster trade. In 1842, the Earl of Carlisle, while visiting New York, said, "everyone seems to be eating oysters all the time."

After 1825, oysters were shipped from the Chesapeake Bay in increasing quantities. New England businessmen began to set up oyster-packing houses in Maryland and Virginia in the 1850s. They sent wagon loads of oysters over land on the Cumberland Road during the winter months to Pittsburg and other points in the Midwest. The Baltimore and Ohio Railroad, running from Baltimore to Wheeling, West Virginia, was completed in 1853 and by 1860, more than three million pounds of oysters flowed westward from nearly sixty packing houses in Baltimore.

The "Great Oyster Craze" began after the American Civil War, while much of the country went through a period of rapid economic expansion and population growth, called the Gilded Age. During this age of unprecedented increases in real wages and wealth, oyster consumption reached obsessive levels.

At the height of the craze, the 1870s and 1880s, oysters could be found in bars, saloons, restaurants, parlors, stalls, lunch rooms, inns and hotels, steamboats, train diners, homes, miners' camps, and on the open range. They were shipped as far as San Francisco and high Rocky Mountain towns by express or special oyster trains. During the peak of the annual raw oyster season, historians estimate that as many as thirty to forty railroad cars of oysters went west from Baltimore daily.

Cowboys at the end of trail drives ate them; lucky miners in high mountain towns ate them; but the heaviest action during the Great Oyster Craze occurred back east, closer to the mother lode of oysters. New York City alone was reported to have 850 oyster parlors in 1874. By the late 1800s, New Yorkers were consuming more than 6 million oysters a day: 660 oysters for every man, woman, and child each year, compared to 60 per capita in London and 26 in Paris.

The other major eastern urban centers, such as Boston and Philadelphia, were not left out of Oyster Mania. In the late 1870s, some 2,419 Philadelphia businesses as well as 158 peddlers and curb-stone stands served oysters. To meet the ferocious demand, a flow of oysters radiated out from New York and Baltimore to inland cities such as Pittsburg, Cincinnati, Cleveland, Detroit, Chicago, Milwaukee, St. Louis, and St. Paul-Minneapolis.

During this period New Orleans and Baltimore were considered the other major oyster markets besides New York and Philadelphia, but they were largely self-sufficient in their own supplies. The post-Reconstruction South did not share in the economic boom of the Gilded Age, yet New Orleans, virtually the only significant market for Louisiana oysters, was not immune to the Great Oyster Craze.

Oyster Saloons speckled New Orleans, especially in and near the French Quarter, although significant numbers of oysters had been consumed in the city since the 1730s. Oyster shucking houses were operating in full swing by 1888. P&J Oyster Company, the oldest continually operating oyster dealer in the U.S., was founded in 1876. Unlike the Northeast, New Orleans did not experience the crumbling of demand after the turn of the century. In 1917, New Orleans still held eighty-three oyster saloons and twenty-nine wholesale oyster dealers.

Felix Rando (left), founder of Felix's Seafood, 1953. (Courtesy John Matranga)

In 1916, Louisiana's Department of Conservation produced Bulletin 1, *The Louisiana Oyster: Its Cultivation and Use*. It extolled the virtues of the state's oysters:

> And now again consider the oyster—from a culinary standpoint. It is a food, inviting, easily digested and high in nutritive value. A family of four may dine sumptuously off of four dozen Louisiana oysters at a top cost for the choicest variety of one-half dollar. Two dozen of these will make a delicious and nourishing *gumbo filet*—a Creole dish of unsurpassed excellence—and the remaining two dozen may be served in a variety of appetizing ways constituting an inviting and satisfying meal.
>
> Very often just a dozen fine, fat, Louisiana oysters added to some left-over of fricasseed chicken, tripe *a la Creole,* or plain boiled rice with tomatoes will constitute a piquant dish sufficient to do ample service for another meal, and at the same time addition of the oysters lends to the "left-over" a savory touch of novelty.
>
> The juice of the oyster, which some have erroneously considered unfit for use, is, on the contrary, a valuable aid to digestion. This fact was definitely proved by the experiments of Henri Coupin, a French scientist. He maintains that the beneficial effects of oysters before meals is due to elements found in the juice. Certainly, many oyster dishes are greatly improved by the addition of the finely flavored liquor, and it is well to know that it can be used not only with safety but with beneficial results.

Currently, the United States is in the middle of an "oyster renaissance." Raw bars that specialize in serving raw shellfish are proliferating and with more variety and improved transportation, lovers of the "Queen of Bivalves" have never had it better.

This surge in oyster popularity is very different than the craze of the nineteenth century. In 1889, the finest and most expensive oysters cost a penny a piece. All classes of people ate them. By the end of the century, they were a "poor-man's food." In 1909 oyster meat cost half the price of chicken, beef, and eggs, and 80 percent of the price of fish. By 1996, about the time of the onset of the renewed interest in oysters, they cost twice as much as fish, four-and-a-half times as much as beef, six times as much as eggs, and nine times the price of chicken.

Oysters are no longer for the poverty-stricken and perhaps the cachet of exclusivity is what is appealing to the senses and pocket books of consumers. Oysters over much of the United States, Louisiana excepted, are labeled, sold, and consumed by location of origin—appellation, to be correct. Oyster connoisseurs rhapsodize over subtle taste differences, exalting in the concept of *terroir*—the taste of the

place from which the food came.

The Oyster Guide by Rowan Jacobson, an internet oyster reference, lists 149 appellations just for U. S. oysters. Some of his descriptions of oyster tastes rival those of wine lovers.

- Malpique oysters: light-bodied and clean on the finish; perfect balance of sweetness, brine, and pickle-like liveliness.
- Kachemak Bay oysters: incredibly clean flavor with lots of

cucumber and a crisp nori kind of snap to them. Salted honeydew, green tea, and apple candy notes linger on the tongue.

- Moonstone oysters: fills your mouth with minerals and brothy umami richness. Copper, iron, clay—it's all there.

Unfortunately, Jacobson, like so many others, lumps all Gulf of Mexico oysters except Apalachicola oysters (including Louisiana's many oysters of many tastes) under the unimaginative appellation, "Gulf Coast," which he describes as follows: "Gulf oysters are usually sold as generic oysters—indicative of a region that pays less attention to the nuances of different raw oysters than to their culinary possibilities. After all, this is the land that invented Oysters Rockefeller, Po'Boys, Barbecued Oysters and myriad other oyster concoctions."

The Long History of the Louisiana Oyster Industry

Oysters have been part of the diet of Louisianans since long before Columbus "discovered" America. Indians discarded the shells of the oysters they ate at their campsites, resulting in the many dozens of prominent shell mounds, called middens, scattered across coastal Louisiana today. Some of these date back 2,000 years. Indians gathered oysters by hand while wading in shallow water or with crude rakes made of two strong poles and vines.

Early European settlers in Louisiana also harvested oysters by wading: a slow, tedious, and often painful method. From hand gathering, the oystermen graduated to the use of long-handled rakes to gather oysters into piles underwater for easy loading into a boat.

As the population of New Orleans grew, the oyster fishery became better developed. By the early nineteenth century, oyster peddlers were aggressively shouting their sales pitches and blowing on conch shells to sell their oysters on street corners. Still, it was difficult to make a full-time living harvesting oysters.

Market demand continued to increase until the mid to late nineteenth century. More fishermen were able to enter the business and

Oyster rakes, used like long handled scissors, were the first tools used by European settlers in Louisiana to gather oysters. (Courtesy Jefferson Parish Yearly Review, 1940)

the oyster industry became a viable part of the Louisiana economy. Even at this time, most of the oysters harvested were gathered ten to thirty miles from the city of New Orleans, and virtually all the supply was consumed in the city and on nearby plantations. All of this harvest of oysters came from wild reefs.

Two different people have been credited with planting the first oysters, some twenty years apart. Some writers credit Luke Jurisich for cultivating oysters in Bayou Cook during the Civil War. Others credit Louis Esponger for first planting seed oysters in 1885 in Whale Bay.

Oyster fishermen became nascent oyster farmers when they began to move small oysters from the marshes east of the Mississippi River to those west of the river. Through observation, they noted that consistently successful oyster spawns east of the river produced densely overcrowded oyster reefs.

Oyster growing conditions were better, however, west of the river for a variety of reasons, including more favorable salinities, better currents, and more abundant food supplies. The small oysters moved from east of the river grew quickly and tasted better in their new homes. Similar developments, of moving small "seed" oysters to better growing waters, were taking place almost simultaneously along the central Louisiana coast.

Shortly before the turn of the nineteenth century, some oystermen began planting cultch material to catch the set of oyster spat. The term "spat" refers to the very tiny oysters that develop from the even smaller, free-living-oyster larvae that have settled down onto hard surfaces to grow. Oyster shells from shucking operations at Oysterville, nine miles north of Port Eads, were used for the cultch material. The shucked oyster meats were eaten locally at Port Eads or packed in milk cans and covered with ice for shipment to New Orleans and beyond.

Some leasing of waterbottoms from parish governments for oyster culture took place as early as the 1850s. But the modern oyster-farming industry did not begin to develop as we know it today until the newly formed Louisiana Oyster Commission began issuing state leases for waterbottoms. The first oyster lease was issued in 1902 for an area on the west side of the Mississippi River, then known as Whale Bay. The lease was issued to Joseph R. Brown of Port Eads, Louisiana.

Around the turn of the twentieth century, oysters sold for three to four dollars a barrel. A barrel contained three bushels of oysters: the equivalent of two sacks today. Oysters were harvested with tongs and nippers (small, lightweight tongs used to pick up individual oysters in clear water) until 1905, when dredges appeared in the fishery.

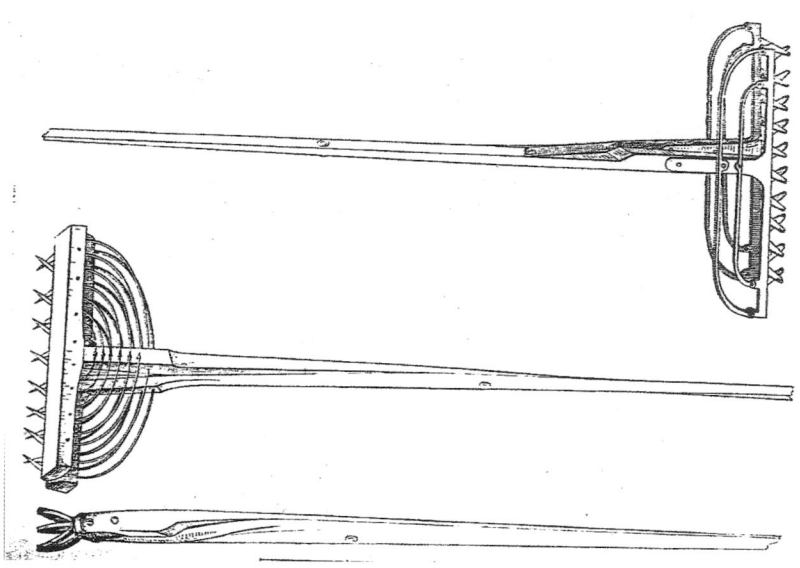

Two versions of oyster rakes and a set of nippers (bottom), which were used to pick up individual oysters. (Courtesy United States Commission of Fish and Fisheries, 1887)

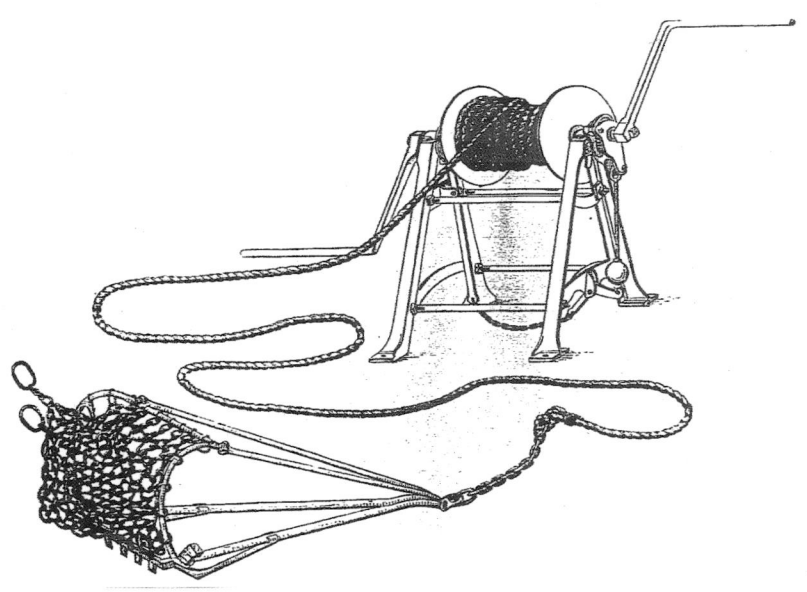

Early oyster dredges were retrieved manually by a windlass set on the deck of the vessel. (Courtesy United States Commission of Fish and Fisheries, 1887)

Legislation in 1904 repealed an 1892 law that prohibited the use of dredges on natural reefs. The earlier law was originally passed because it was thought that the use of dredges provided an unfair advantage to some oystermen. These early dredges were retrieved with hand-operated winches. Within ten years, power dredges came into use and are still used today

The turn of the century also saw engine-powered boats replacing sailing luggers, a shift that was complete by 1920. Sailing luggers typically carried one Mediterranean-style, nearly square sail hung from a long yard.

At the time of the Civil War, three major commercial grades of oysters were produced: steam cannery, raw shop, and counter trade. Steamers or steam cannery oysters were the poorest grade, often small, poorly shaped, and harvested in dense clumps that made hand-shucking difficult. They were steam-opened and the meats were shaken loose.

Most steam cannery oysters packed in New Orleans came from huge reef areas east of the Mississippi River, especially the area known as the Louisiana Marsh. Many of these oysters, often called "coon oysters," were also shipped to Mississippi Gulf Coast canneries. In Louisiana, Morgan City and Houma were also prime locations for canning steam oysters, as well as for the sale of raw-shop oysters.

The outer and the inner boats of these four oyster boats docked at the Barracks Street Wharf in New Orleans are equipped with windlass dredges. The two inner boats hauled hand-tonged oysters to market, 1930s. (Courtesy Ralph "Buddy" Pausina)

Seed oysters were carried to oyster beds in hand-poled wooden skiffs and spread with shovels for further growth. (Courtesy Jefferson Parish Yearly Review, 1940)

Oysters being unloaded from a sail-powered vessel by bucket on a pulley at Empire, Louisiana, in the early 1900s. Left to right on deck of vessel, Adrian Bulot, Alphonse Galmiche, Paul Bulot, unidentified, Paul Dazet. (Courtesy Enola Dazet Balliviero)

Another name for steam oysters in New Orleans was "basin oysters," because of their arrival in New Orleans by way of the Basin and the New Basin Canals. The Basin Canal extended from Bayou St. John, along Orleans Avenue, to just north of the French Quarter.

The Basin Canal was replaced by the larger New Basin Canal, which started at Lake Pontchartrain and extended southward where West End and Pontchartrain Boulevards are today, turned toward the business district, and ended in a turning basin at the present site of the Superdome. The New Basin Canal was filled in the late 1940s and early 1950s. Only a remnant now exists, marked by the U. S. Coast Guard Station and lighthouse at West End.

Raw-shop oysters were larger and better-shaped oysters, more suitable for being shucked by hand. In some cases, these oysters were minimally cultivated by the clumps of oysters being separated by hand on boats and spread over a hard bottom for more growth. After shucking, these oysters were typically sold locally or placed in cans, packed in ice, and shipped to nearby markets.

The best class of oysters was counter stock, used in the half-shell trade. They were always marketed in Louisiana as Bayou Cook oysters, because Bayou Cook was the location where high-quality oysters were first grown. These oysters were heavily cultivated and when nearly market size, they were moved to saline "fattening grounds" to become plump and salty. The oysters on these grounds

Oyster luggers clustered at the Fruit Landing in the Basin Canal. (Joseph Pennell, 1882)

were quite often protected from attacks from black drum fish by the use of wooden fences.

Counter-stock oysters came into New Orleans by a different route than that used for transporting oysters for steaming. By various distributaries, the luggers entered the Mississippi River; then they traveled upriver and docked at the city's Picayune Tier (lugger landing) near the French Market.

Before the 1880s, most of the oysters reaching New Orleans were consumed locally. Until the turn of the century, Louisiana oysters carried a poor reputation nationally. This was because only the cheapest and poorest-quality oysters were shipped out of state, and all the best oysters were used to satisfy local demand.

The development of the oyster industry played a major role in the creation of what are today known as the Louisiana Department of Wildlife and Fisheries and the Louisiana Wildlife and Fisheries Commission. The very first step taken in wildlife conservation in Louisiana dates back to 1857, when the Louisiana Legislature passed a law to protect game birds in the state. Control of this law was later given to parish police juries.

The developing Louisiana oyster industry prompted the next major conservation steps. In 1870, fear of oyster reef depletion caused the Legislature to close the oyster season from April 1 to September 15 annually. In 1871, the Legislature changed the closure to May 1 to

September 15. Then, in 1886, the Legislature passed Act 106, which divided the state into three oyster districts and authorized the governor to appoint an oyster commissioner for each district. The act also authorized the leasing of up to three acres of waterbottoms by individuals or corporations. Act 110 in 1892 increased the amount of waterbottom allowable for leasing to ten acres per person.

More importantly, Act 110 also abolished the oyster commissioner system, declared oysters to be the property of each individual parish, and provided that only parish residents could harvest them. This caused tremendous conflicts because citizens in one parish commonly crossed parish lines to harvest oysters in another, and parish boundaries are not marked on the water. The conflicts led to the creation of a legislative investigative commission in 1900.

Their report to the Legislature in 1902 resulted in the passage of Act 153, which created the five-member Oyster Commission of Louisiana, which held statewide control of the oyster industry. This commission later became the Oyster, Waterbottoms, and Seafood Division, the first and oldest division of what is now the Louisiana Department of Wildlife and Fisheries.

Lugger Landing on the bank of the Mississippi River in New Orleans in 1906. (Courtesy Eva Vujnovich)

In 1908, the Louisiana Legislature passed Act 278, creating the Board of Commissioners for the Protection of Birds, Game, and Fish. The board was given the authority to appoint game wardens. Funding for the wardens was provided by requiring hunters to purchase hunting licenses.

In 1910, the Oyster Commission and the Board of Commissioners for the Protection of Birds, Game, and Fish were merged by Act 265. In 1912, with Act 127, all fish and wildlife activities were consolidated under the "Conservation Commission of Louisiana" as a department of state government. Act 105 in 1918 created the Department of Conservation under a Commissioner of Conservation. Commission members were appointed to four-year terms by the governor.

In November 1944, a constitutional amendment was approved creating the Louisiana Wild Life and Fisheries Commission, which later became the Louisiana Department of Wild Life and Fisheries in 1952, with a separate Wild Life and Fisheries Commission. The Legislature of Louisiana gave the new agency, created in 1944, the responsibility of protecting, conserving, and propagating the wildlife of Louisiana. The first Commissioner, John G. Appel, established

James N. McConnell (second from left), director of the Division of Oysters and Waterbottoms in the newly created Louisiana Wild Life and Fisheries Commission, visits oystermen George Vujnovich (second from right) and Pete Vujnovcich (right) on their oyster boat, mid-1940s. (Courtesy Eva Vujnovich)

six major programs: 1) control of the water hyacinth, 2) control of predators, 3) enlarged fish rescue and restocking programs, 4) enlarged education and public relations programs, 5) enlarged enforcement programs, and 6) obtaining public shooting grounds.

Finally in 1976, the name of the agency was changed to what it is now, the Louisiana Department of Wildlife and Fisheries. This long history makes the department one of the oldest conservation bodies in the nation.

In May 1953, the Louisiana Oyster Dealers and Growers Association held an oyster shucking contest on Canal Street in New Orleans to promote summertime consumption of oysters. Note future New Orleans Mayor Vic Schiro with his hand to his forehead in the center foreground. (Courtesy George Barisich)

Family Pride

It's six days before Christmas and Capt. Pete Vujnovich, Jr., has an order. The oyster buyer wants 150 mini-sacks, which Pete calls "bucket sacks" because they hold a heaping five-gallon bucket of oysters. He doesn't have a lot of time. The buyer wants them by Monday evening, leaving him only two days to dredge, so he has enlisted his brother Frank Vujnovich to pair up with him to fill the order.

It's cold and crisp. The jet stream has pushed a polar air mass down past Port Sulphur in Plaquemines Parish, where Pete's boat, the *Capt. Pete* is nosed to the bank next to Frank's boat, the *Miss Eva.* The fifty-four-foot boats are named after the brothers' parents. Their late father Capt. Pete Vujnovich, Sr., had developed near-legendary status within the Louisiana oyster farming industry while he was still alive.

In spite of the brilliant sun, I involuntarily shiver against the north

The two oyster tidy luggers were snugged up to the bank on the cold crisp morning.

wind and 44 degree weather when I step out of my truck. I think about the warm watch cap packed in my duffel bag, while I walk quickly to the boat. Pete is already there to greet me, bright-eyed and bushy-tailed at 7:30 in the morning. "Good morning," he greets me cheerily.

"It's cold," was my reply. "Yeah, and it's a real low tide, too," he countered. Successive cold fronts had pushed much of the water out of the marshes and into the Gulf of Mexico. The retreating water has exposed extensive mud flats along the banks, which in turn are "perfuming" the air with sulfurous smells. The odor, offensive to some, is redolent to me of Louisiana's rich salt marshes.

I like it.

After bringing my gear on board, I have time to kill. Pete's helper for the trip, his twenty-one-year old son Cullen, and brother Frank haven't arrived yet. While Pete tidies up the already neat boat, I admire the two trim and well-painted vessels. Both are instantly recognizable as oyster luggers.

Their cabins are set as far as possible to the rear of the vessels, leaving a large open work area in front of each cabin. The low-slung working decks are completely shaded by canvas awnings tightly stretched over pipe frames. The oyster-boat-look is completed by removable wooden pin boards set horizontally along the rail-less edges of the boats' decks.

Pete introduces me to Cullen when he arrives at 8:00 AM. "I named him 'Cullen' after 'culling oysters.' Get it?" "Wow," I think to myself, "Oysters run deep in this family." Cullen is six feet, two inches tall, 190 pounds, and athletically built, as he should be. He attends LSU-Alexandria under a baseball scholarship. Home for Christmas break, he explains that he came on this trip to help his dad as well as to make a little extra money.

The two make a trip to a nearby grocery store to get the few provisions for this trip and I am left to pass time on the boat, so I take in the scenery. The air is full of birds. Brown pelicans soar over and around the boat like bombers, shepherded, fighter-like, by more agile sea gulls. It's hard to believe that anything so ungainly on the water as a pelican can be so graceful on the wing.

My bird watching is interrupted by the simultaneous return of the two men and the appearance of Frank Vujnovich and his two sons Timmy and Jeremy. With five sets of hands, both boats are quickly loaded with supplies and we are finally ready to go. It's almost 9:00 AM and we have a solid three hour run before the first dredge hits the water.

The tide has fallen another inch and it seems like more than half the length of the boat is grounded on mud flat. Pete revs the *Capt. Pete's* diesel engine and powers the boat forward, backward, and side-to-side to loosen the boat from the mud. Slowly, almost imperceptibly at first, the boat creeps to the rear as the muck loses its grip on the hull.

The *Miss Eva* follows. We are off, traveling out Freeport Sulphur Company Canal, heading into the Barataria Bay complex. Our destination is Redfish Bay, a small bay near Hackberry Bay. Oystermen lease the use of waterbottoms from the state for their oyster farms. Pete owns leases throughout the Barataria Bay system and manages these, as well as leases held by a business acquaintance, Carolyn Falgout.

Once in open water, the two boats run parallel to each other, with the *Miss Eva* slightly to the rear of the *Capt. Pete.* The green water reflects the blue of the sky and Frank's snow-white lugger looks like a wedding cake skimming its surface.

Peter Vujnovich sits pensively at the helm of his boat. He doesn't really know what to expect. It is only his second full trip since the BP oil spill of 2010 turned the fishing world in coastal Louisiana upside down. He has checked his leases periodically. He knows that many of his oysters, 70 percent by his estimation, are dead—killed by the

The Miss Eva *shines brightly in the brilliant morning sun.*

months-long diversion of freshwater from the Mississippi River. The diversions were the state's attempt to push back crude oil from the interior marshes.

He also knows that oil at one time or another passed over the surface of another 20 percent or so of his leases. These oysters aren't dead, but Pete is hesitant to harvest them right now. Today and tomorrow he will work in the thin sliver of area north of the oiled areas and south of what was decimated by freshwater.

Cullen, like young deck hands on any fishing boat do whenever they have a break, crawls into a bunk. Pete watches him and grins. I ask Pete if he is interested in becoming an oysterman. "It's in his best interest to go to school," he replies, "because it will give him options. But if either he or my other son [Peter III] are interested, they are welcome to get in.

"In my generation, sons were expected to carry on in the business. I started actively working on weekends and in the summers in about the eighth grade. After graduating from Brother Martin High School I went to college at Southeastern and majored in biology. I took all the biology classes I could and then I lost interest. I didn't come for English, foreign languages, or history. I quit when I lost interest.

"To me, college was only a delay to the inevitable. I was gonna end up on the boat, no matter what. When I was thirteen, I surrendered to the idea that I was gonna fish oysters. I spent thirty-one days straight on a boat. When one boat went in with a load, I would be put on the other.

"When the boat going in pulled away, I would be literally crying.

"Pops [his father Pete Vujnovich Sr.] loved it out here. He loved oysters with a passion. I like oyster farming, but I don't love it with the same passion that he did. For years, I wondered 'what if,' but it turned out to be a blessing."

Much of the intensity of the first twenty-five years of his oystering life, he explains, came from the pressures of producing a supply of oysters for Capt. Pete's Oyster House, the family shucking business. Peter Sr. founded the business to create a market for the oysters that they produced, but the shucking house's demand for oysters began to drive the fishery, rather than the other way around.

Hurricane Katrina closed the business and Pete Sr., began to come out on the boat a lot less. "I took over. There was more responsibility, but more freedom. I can take a day off when I want to. Before, I had to fish constantly to supply the shucking house.

"Since 2005, I am a lot more content with what this way of life offers.

The majority of days I really like what I do—now when the weather is kicking butt and the resource [oyster numbers] isn't there—that's the miserable side of life."

At 11:30 AM he retrieves a package of bologna from the boat's propane refrigerator and loaf of Bunny Bread. He washes down a couple of sandwiches with swigs from his fourth or fifth Diet Coke of the morning, lights a cigarette, and ruminates on his plans.

Cullen emerges from hibernation and grabs a bite to eat, while Pete methodically pulls on his cold-weather gear. Dressed for combat, he eases back on the engine throttle, and then fills out his harvest log, noting the exact area to be harvested and the time harvest begins. Health regulations demand strict recordkeeping on oyster boats.

He turns the rudder sharply to port, slips on a set of dark, protective goggles, and steps out on deck. While the vessel idles in a circle, he sets up baskets and buckets for the culled oysters and gets burlap sacks out of the hold. In the near distance, the *Miss Eva* is doing the same circular dance, as her crew readies her for fishing.

Finally, he pulls on the heavy, rubberized gloves that most oystermen seem to use. He walks to one side of the boat and man-handles the heavy iron dredge overboard with a wild clatter of chains and clang of metal against metal. He repeats the process with the dredge on the opposite side of the boat.

Recordkeeping is an important part of being a modern oysterman.

Oyster dredges are simple but sturdy and effective.

Medium-sized oysters destined for the half-shell trade are the men's main target for the day.

Bundled against the cold, Pete wrestles the first oyster dredge overboard by himself.

It's 12:30 PM and we are fishing. Pete has located his reef in what seems like featureless open water without using a GPS or any other navigational aid. "I just know my area," he says with a grin.

He takes his position, facing rearward, at the front wheel, which is a set of controls and small captain's wheel on a console on the bow. Two power drums at the base of the console hold the chain used to retrieve the oyster dredges. Each dredge consists of a frame, the bulk of which is called a neck. The bottom is toothed to dislodge oysters from the reef, causing them to tumble up and into a bag made of steel rings and knotted rope.

The chain from the drums is strung through a pair of blocks (pulleys), and then over a pair of aluminum culling tables set on each side of the boat. When a dredge is retrieved, the winch pulls it up tightly to the bar over the table. The bag is then turned inside-out manually to empty its contents onto the table beneath it.

Pete has the boat's rudder locked in one direction, making the boat work in lazy, partially overlapping circles. After perhaps ten minutes, the first dredge is retrieved, emptied, and shoved back overboard to continue fishing. Pete and Cullen immediately begin culling the catch with small culling hatchets. Both the peen side and the blade side of the hatchet are used as the men see fit.

Clusters are broken into singles to retrieve salable oysters. Medium-sized oysters, estimated by Pete to be three to four-years old and their prime target for the day, are tossed into a five-gallon bucket set by each table. Larger oysters, aged five years and older, end up in large wire baskets set on deck. These oysters, destined for shucking, will be put into larger burlap sacks. Empty shells and small oysters are tossed back overboard onto the reef as the men cull the catch.

Pete works the front end of the tables so as to be near the front wheel. He is constantly aware of the boat's circling course and adjusts its track often. Cullen, who works the rear of the tables, has the responsibility of sacking the oysters when the buckets or baskets are full and stacking the sacks on the deck near the cabin.

After they empty the dredge the first time, I look to Pete for his assessment on the effects of the freshwater diversion. It's an unhappy okay.

"I see about 30 percent mortality. The most we could get out of this is maybe a month's work, then I would have to let it sit six months before getting two more weeks. If I thought that I could get better from my other areas, I would work them and let this set."

When they finish culling the table on one side, they immediately retrieve the other dredge and go to work on its catch on the other table.

Pete culls oysters at the front of the table near his boat controls, while Cullen culls and sacks at the back end of the table.

Cullen samples a fresh one, cold from the winter water.

This is the pace they would keep up for two days. It is relentless. Only when a dredge flipped over and came up empty would they get a free moment. Then, Cullen would dash into the cabin for a cupcake or Pete would pull out another Diet Coke to go with his ever-present cigarette.

The deck of an oyster boat is a noisy place to work. The steady clink, clink, clink of metal hatchets on shells, the thunder of dredges coming in and crashing back, the avalanche of oyster shells on the metal tables, the rattle of chains, and the oysters clunking into buckets and clanging into metal baskets is unceasing.

All the while, the boat slowly churns in overlapping circles. In the distance, the *Miss Eva* is doing the same. Pete constantly jumps from the culling table to the wheel to adjust course. Sometimes the boat's circles are lazy loops; other times the vessel turns so sharply that it seems to spin dizzyingly in one spot.

Cullen empties bucket after bucket into mini-sacks and slowly but steadily they start to accumulate—six sacks, eight sacks, ten sacks. Burlap mini-sacks are specially made for the oyster trade, but the large sacks are recycled burlap sacks in which coffee beans were imported for Louisiana's coffee roasting industry.

Hands and hatchets work in a blur, almost too fast for the eye to see. One hand expertly tosses the clusters to expose their vulnerable points, while the other hand flips the hatchet from blade to peen and back again and seems to unerringly hit the right spot in the cluster. At several points, sparks actually fly off Pete's hatchet blade.

This isn't the younger man's first rodeo, either. Cullen is as fast as his father. I wonder out loud how they never hit their hand with the blade of the hatchet. "You hit your hands a few times," Cullen murmurs, "you learn quick."

Periodically one of the men will pry open an oyster with his hatchet and sample the wares, unembellished by anything other than sea water. Pete knows his leases. Where we started at noon, the oysters had only a hint of salt. At 3:15 PM and only a few hundred yards from where we started, Pete suggested I try another. "They should be saltier."

It was, and so was the second one. He explains that a nearby marsh island changes the flow of the water and effectively alters the salinity by several points.

The sacks keep piling up—twenty-eight sacks, then twenty-nine, then thirty.

Finally at 5:10 PM, with darkness descending, Pete calls it a day. Their backs are kinked and their clothes are grimy, but they have knocked out forty-one little sacks and three big ones.

Pete chugs the boat to two stray pilings, to which Cullen ties the boat. It is near dark and a huge, platinum, winter, near-full moon is rising overhead. It's beautiful, but it's still cold; the wind is still from the north at ten to fifteen miles per hour.

The Vujnovich crews visit as the boats tie up for the night (left to right, Pete Jr., Cullen, Jeremy, Frank, and Tim).

When the dredge is snugged to the lip on the table, the two men grab the rings on the bag and deftly flick the bag inside-out, emptying its catch. Then they push the dredge back overboard to resume fishing.

One dredge is pulled by chains on each side of the boat. The dredges are emptied alternately.

Frank pulls the *Miss Eva* alongside the *Capt. Pete* and the crews secure the two vessels together. The two captains compare fishing notes while their cousin-sons visit and tease each other.

The *Miss Eva* has made fifty-six mini-sacks and eight big ones. But the boat's generator is down for the count with a leaking freeze plug. Pete retreats to the cabin and stamps his oyster tags. Each sack must have a tag on it that lists the harvest area, the date of harvest, and the harvester's identification number.

As the glow from Grand Isle lights up the southern horizon, Pete sears rib eye steaks in a frying pan for supper. In the *Miss Eva,* the menu entrée is duck stew.

The next morning we awaken to a beautiful sight. The slanting rays of the rising sun are chromatically lighting up the vast tract of marsh grass waving in the breeze near us like a golden field of wheat. The water between the boat and the large island glitters as if strewn with diamonds.

Pete puffs a cigarette and sips his morning Diet Coke silently. He sighs and comments with resignation about the loss of Louisiana's marshlands. The pilings we are tied to were once the wharf of a camp, now long gone. The camp was on land; now the pilings are 300 yards away from the nearest land.

But the time for reflection is short. The men slip on their dirty outerwear togs and untie the boats. The dredges are hurled overboard with shattering clangs and another day begins.

It's a beautiful, if chilly, morning. The wind laid down some overnight. In the brilliant morning light, the white *Miss Eva* shimmers brightly in the distance as it does its circular dance. Nearby, a solitary crabber in a Carolina Skiff is running his traps set just off the edge of the reef.

As the *Capt. Pete* droned in its own circles, every dredge seemed to come up with more oysters than the day before. The oystermen's hands move in harmony with each other. Every strike of the hatchet on a cluster being spun by the other hand strikes in exactly the right spot to break apart the agglomeration. Clink—clink—clink.

As I watch the men work, my mind wanders and I begin pondering whose Christmas festivities these half-shell wonders will grace. They will only see the oysters, not the dredgery (one of Pete's favorite made-up words), that went into getting the oysters to their tables.

The sacks rapidly accumulate—fifty-five mini-sacks were stacked up well before 10:00 AM. By 11:00 AM, when the *Miss Eva* comes coasting up, the total has grown to seventy-three mini-sacks and five large sacks. Frank has ninety-five mini-sacks and fifteen big sacks. Combined, they have enough to meet their order and plenty to share with family and friends for Christmas.

Both the blade and the peen of the hatchets are used with incredible speed to cull the catch.

Clusters are quickly separated into singles, which are kept if large enough, and small oysters or empty shells, which are returned overboard to the reef.

Slowly but steadily, full sacks accumulate.

Pete and Cullen clean the working deck, with Cullen on the deck hose and Pete wielding a long handled brush. They shed their muddy, cold-weather clothes and retreat to the shelter of the cabin for the run back to Port Sulphur.

On the slow ride in, Pete talks about what it takes to be a Louisiana oyster farmer. He quickly admits that the actual work of harvesting oysters borders on "dredgery," (his word again) but says that his real enjoyment comes from managing the oyster resources on a grand scale over his multitude of leases.

"Every year I have a limited amount of resource. Some years it's more abundant than other years. I rotate pressure on the resource between the leases to allow oysters to grow. Also, I transplant oysters between my leases for better survival and growth."

He explains that only about 5 percent of what he catches for sale comes from wild or public reefs, formally called "seed grounds." But, he does depend on seed grounds for 25 to 30 percent of his seed oysters: small oysters less than three inches in diameter. His heavy reliance on his own reefs as a source of seed oysters is unusual in modern oyster culture.

Pete's oyster leases are scattered throughout the Barataria Bay system. On those leases in high-salinity waters, oysters grow faster and prettier (rounder, fatter, and better tasting). But seed oysters don't do well on these reefs because of oyster drills (carnivorous snails), crabs, and black drum.

Conversely, in lower salinity waters, spat set (larval oyster fallout on hard surfaces) is poor, but those that do set have a high survival rate. So he rotates oysters from reef to reef as part of his management scheme. Seeing what is happening and reacting demands year-round attention.

Besides rotating small seed oysters from his high-salinity reefs to those in less salty waters, Pete harvests and transports seed oysters from public seed grounds in September and October. Even though the seed grounds east of the Mississippi River produce a larger volume of seed, Pete concentrates his harvest in Hackberry Bay.

Harvesting seed oysters from the east side of the river means trips through the Mississippi River locks at Empire and Ostrica, a three day ordeal. The longer seed oysters sit on the deck of a boat before being bedded, the weaker the oysters become and the more vulnerable they are to high mortality.

But predation is only a part of the challenge that oyster farmers face. Pete ticks the others off: oil and gas activity, theft, crew problems, health regulations, and too much freshwater.

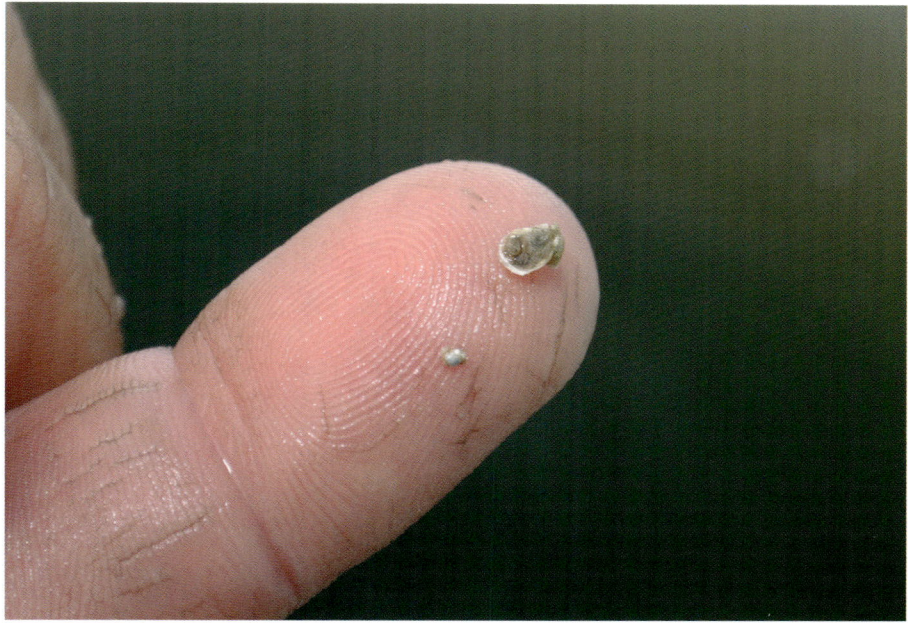

To survive, tiny oysters, called spat, must find hard surfaces on which to attach themselves, as well as the right water salinities.

Oystermen share coastal waters with oil and gas production activities and, according to him, they get along "pretty good." He gestures with both arms and says, "I don't want to sail this big boat," in reference to the fact that the lugger is diesel-powered. "But boats do get out of channels and a big tug can churn up a reef and destroy its integrity. It can be impossible to repair if the boat churns through the hard crust down to soupier sediment layers."

He notes that oil and gas activity in the coastal zone is down in recent years, but some dredging of channels still occurs, although the permitting process now allows input from leaseholders to suggest less damaging routes.

Theft of oysters from private leases was a serious problem when oysters hit a high of nearly $30 a sack prior to the late 1980s. All sorts of people stole oysters, from those with big dredge boats to cooners in small, high-speed outboard motor-propelled boats. Cooners harvest oysters by getting overboard in shallow waters and pulling oysters off the bottom by hand.

Theft led to shoot-outs on the water and camp burnings. Pete still believes that the Vujnovich family camp was burned by oyster thieves whom the family was trying to keep off their leases.

Capt. Pete Vujnovich Jr., describes how oyster farming and oil exploration share the same waters.

He attributes much of the abatement of theft to stiffer penalties, the creation of the Oyster Strike Force within the Louisiana Department of Wildlife and Fisheries Enforcement Division, and strong water patrols by the Plaquemines Parish and Lafourche Parish Sheriffs' Offices.

The difficulty of obtaining crewmen for oyster boats is a more recent problem, acknowledges Pete. "The Frenchmen [Cajuns] on Bayou Lafourche are almost out of the business and Takos [Croatians such as himself] are on the way out. It looks like it will be almost all Mexicans."

Pete is also concerned for the oyster market because of health regulations. "The uncertainties of regulations has definitely affected market demand. We were doing real well until health authorities required warnings on raw oyster consumption because of *Vibrio vulnificus.* Negative publicity hurts and no one knows what is coming yet."

But Pete's deepest concerns for the future are over freshwater. Some years, high river discharge and strong local rains can so lower the salinity of coastal waters that significant oyster mortality occurs. But that has always been a natural risk.

What has changed is the risk of freshwater damage to oyster leases from man-made diversions of Mississippi River water into coastal marshes. These diversions are promoted as a method of funneling river sediments into wetlands to offset land loss caused by subsidence and erosion.

Pete estimates that 70 percent of the oysters on his combined leases were killed by the 2010 freshwater diversions operated during the BP oil spill.

"Up until the BP oil spill, Davis Ponds [Freshwater Diversion] has tremendously helped the oyster industry," he begins. "It stabilized the industry so that it isn't moving inward toward closure lines. If the old northward trends had continued, oyster populations would have ended up largely within closed areas that are polluted by being close to civilization.

"Controlled freshwater diversions can keep the oysterman working in more historical areas and keep predators at bay. An oysterman knows what to anticipate in managing his seeding operation.

"The drawbacks are that if they are improperly operated, they can cause massive oyster mortality. That's what happened following the BP spill. Opening the diversions wide open may have had some validity in keeping the oil out. We will never know, but it was an understandable attempt.

"But 70 percent of my resource on my leases was killed, all because of freshwater, not oil. I expect that it will take three years to recover to a normal pattern and five years to reach peak production. My biggest fear is that they will build freshwater diversions so big that they destroy the oyster industry."

Still, he seems somewhat sanguine about the future. "I am confident that the oyster industry will exist for my lifetime, but things will

Oysters from the two boats are loaded by conveyor into a refrigerated truck that will head for New Orleans in time for Christmas deliveries.

change. I can see that with continued [coastal] erosion we may not be able to maintain salinities for oyster culture. Freshwater diversion will not be enough.

"Hatchery technology and off-bottom [oyster] culture may offset some of the negative effects of either or both coastal erosion and freshwater diversion. But the most important factor is if the oyster industry is considered in freshwater diversion operation as a part of coastal restoration as a whole.

"Developing a lease is a lifetime commitment. I am reaping the benefits of reef areas my grandfather developed. I am proud of my industry, but the majority of my pride is the tradition of my family and their part in the industry.

"Other people work just as hard as we do, but there is a mystique in oysters. We are a focus of attention and I am proud of the role my family has played—absolutely!"

The Capt. Pete *looks for its berth at the end of the trip.*

Tako-Tako

In rural south Louisiana, virtually every individual and ethnic group carries an affectionate nickname. Thus it is with the Croatians, who so dominate the oyster industry of extreme southeastern Louisiana. They are known as "Takos."

The nickname apparently originates from an idiom in their language. In the days before fishermen had radios to communicate between oyster boats, their skippers would communicate by hand signals and voice as they passed each other.

The most frequent question, naturally, was how the other's catch was. Fishermen being fishermen in any language, they didn't want to admit to a real good catch, nor did they want to lie. So they commonly replied "tako-tako," meaning "okay-okay" or "so-so." Cajun and Anglo fishermen, on hearing the word repeated so often, hung the appellation on the group and it stuck.

Several thousand people of Croatian heritage live in Plaquemines Parish and the greater New Orleans area. Several well-known restaurants such as Drago's, Crescent City Steakhouse, Uglesich's,

Four Croatians heading by boat to the Tesvich oyster camp in Plaquemines Parish in the 1940s. The basket contains a jug of wine made from grapes and raisins fermented at the camp. The man on the left is Gaspar Seput, an oyster worker for the family. The man on the right is Anthony Pausina, a Tesvich relative. The women are unidentified. (Courtesy Domenica Cibilich and John Tesvich)

Bozo's, and Mandich's were or are owned by Croatians. Croatian surnames also appear in all the professions and in government, but nowhere has their impact been so great as in the Louisiana oyster industry. Luke Jurisich, who settled at Bayou Creek in 1855, is often called the father of the Croatian oyster fishery. Pete Vujnovich, Sr., who was born in the Dalmatian village of Sucuraj in 1923 and moved to Louisiana in 1931, is still revered as the oyster industry's modern father and conscience, even after his death in 2008.

The Louisianans who now call themselves Croatians, or occasionally Dalmatians, used to refer to themselves as "Slavonians" or Yugoslavs until the 1991 to 2001 Yugoslav wars that rent apart the former Socialist Federal Republic of Yugoslavia. The wars were bitter ethnic conflicts that affected even the Croatians in Louisiana, many of whom have maintained close ties to their relatives in the old country.

Although some Dalmatian sailors settled in Louisiana in the 1700s, Croatian immigration to Louisiana to fish for oysters did not ramp up until the 1840s. Immigration to the U.S. peaked between 1900 and 1914 and Louisiana was a center of Croatian immigration. Many immigrants were single men who had to leave their families behind until they earned enough to bring them here.

The contributions of the Croatian immigrants were recognized early. An 1892 newspaper article reported that in the Bayou Cook area of Barataria Bay, "bedding [of oysters] is done here almost exclusively

Pete Vujnovich, Sr., on left, with Ivo Ivovich, Capt. George Vujnovich (his father), and Milos Vujnovich (his brother) on his right. (Courtesy Eva Vujnovich)

by the 'Fajoli' [fajioli: a meatless pasta and bean dish] eating sons of Austria, commonly called 'Packos.'" F. C. Zacharie, in an 1897 Fish Commission Bulletin stated that Louisiana oystermen were "mostly uneducated Austrians from the Slavonic provinces; commonly known as Takoes."

Croatian oystermen, single or married, typically spent much of the year living in stilt houses (called oyster camps) over the marsh or water near their oyster grounds in Plaquemines Parish. The women often moved to Empire or even New Orleans for part of the year so their children could attend school. The Plaquemines Parish towns of Empire, Buras, Olga, and Port Sulphur were largely populated by Croatians.

Before road transportation improved, Croatian oystermen would run their slow lugger boats up the Mississippi River to New Orleans and unload their catches on the city's wharves and the river bank. Now, even though their boats are faster, oyster catches are transported to the city from the water-world below it by truck.

Croatian families, such as John Vesich's, often lived in remote oyster camps in the marsh, ca. 1933-1934. (Courtesy Eva Vujnovich)

Croatian settlers' lives revolved around oyster camps and boats. (left to right Neda Jurisich, Gloria Cvitanovich, unknown, Antonin Taliancich and Eva Jurisich) (Courtesy George Barasich)

The majority of Croatian surnames end in "ich" and are patronyms. This means that they were named after a male ancestor. For example the surname of "Tomich" means a "descendent of Toma (Thomas)" and "Adamic" means a "descendent of Adam." Similar English patronyms would be Thompson and Adamson.

The foundations for Croatian cooking are good olive oil, onions, and garlic. Croatians are famous for loving spaghetti, and oyster spaghetti may be their biggest culinary contribution to Louisiana. Croatians are also proud of their baked goods including hrostula, a Dalmatian cookie, and a round lemon-flavored, sweet bread called kolach.

Paul Zibilich Co.
INCORPORATED

Banner Oyster and Fish Depot
"THE HOUSE OF QUALITY AND SERVICE"

OYSTERS OUR SPECIALTY
FRESH FISH, SHRIMP, CRABS, FROGS,
TURTLES AND VEGETABLES

RED STORE BUILDING
N. PETERS AND ST. PHILIP STS

PHONES MAIN
6702

P. O. BOX
1281

NEW ORLEANS

August 7, 1929

Mr. Rado Hihar,
Empire, La.

Dear Mr. Hihar:

Your communication of the 5th instant advising
that you have some oysters that grew on reefs and that
you would like for us to handle same reached us promptly.
In reply thereto will say that as you requested the writer
to send you some sacks same was done, and we were somewhat
surprised at not receiving sample shipments from you.

When your letter reached us we made investigation
and find that two shipments of 5 bundles of sacks each
have been on the Launch Protector for the past two weeks,
and recentl, Marianne Barbalich said he would see that these
sacks reaches your fisheries.

Please do not feel as though this matter has not
received our attention because such is not the case. As
explained above the delay in these sacks reaching you rests
with some one else and not with our office.

Just as soon as we receive the sample shipment
we will advise you further relative to our handling same.

Yours very truly,

Paul Zibilich Co., Incorporated

PACKERS AND SHIPPERS OF THE FAMOUS CYPRIAN BAY AND
RENOWNED BAYOU COOK, FOUR BAYOU, PORT EADS AND SALINE OYSTERS.

Croatians were prominent oyster dealers as well as oyster farmers.

A Frenchman's Tale

The dapper, beret-wearing man sits at the kitchen table in his Golden Meadow, Louisiana, home. Still handsome at seventy-three, he has an engaging smile, in spite of being in the midst of a family business crisis. Capt. Wilbert Collins speaks with the musical Cajun accent of Bayou Lafourche. "This is the first time in over one hundred years that the Collins family doesn't have oysters to sell. Sixty years for me, and then grandfather and father."

It is nine months since the BP oil spill. Fresh Mississippi River waters introduced through the Davis Ponds Freshwater Diversion Structure in an attempt to hold back the oil have decimated his family's oyster bed populations.

He goes on. "It's very disappointing—I don't have no big words. When you've got family that was depending on Collin's Oyster Company—it's very sad. My sons, Nick and Levi, depend on the company. My grandfather, Levi Colllins Sr., named the company Grand Isle Oyster Company. I bought it out from Daddy in 1985 and changed its name."

Wilbert Collins stands behind a rusting dredge on his idle oyster boat, the Capt. Wilbert.

I interrupt to ask how, with the name "Collins," could he be French Cajun? "Oh, I'm Cajun. *Je parler Français.* One great grandfather was Scottish. He left Europe through France to come to Bayou Lafourche. He married a Cajun girl and every generation after that married a Cajun.

"My grandfather began fishing oysters—all tongs in those days. He used to make good oysters by planting with tongs. His first reefs were near Brush Island in Timbalier Bay. I believe that was about the time they [the state] first started leasing. But he got out for a while and was a sheriff's deputy in the late 20s. Then he moved to Cheniere [a "suburb" of modern Grand Isle] and started leasing leases. That was the beginning of Grand Isle Oyster Company."

Collins explains that all the oyster work was done on small skiffs. They had one boat with an engine that pulled two tonging skiffs full of small, seed oysters from Sister Lake to their leases for planting. The men moved the skiffs while tonging and shoveling seed by using push poles. "It was entirely different than today."

Levi Collins Sr., died in the 1960s at seventy-six years old, and Levi Jr., his son and Wilbert's father, took over the business. "He was an oysterman all his life," said Wilbert. "When he wasn't oystering, like in shrimp season, he would seine shrimp. I did that one time when I was little and then it was all over—trawls came out."

Wilbert's father sold oysters to "big boats" twice a week, which freighted them to market. Later, trucks came twice a week by gravel road to Cheniere to haul oysters to Baton Rouge. "It was hard in those days. They had a lot of oysters and a lot of oystermen," he recalls. The earliest price that he can remember was $2.50 a sack.

"When I started in the business, we retailed at the camp in Cheniere and at our house in Golden Meadow," he said. "I've been selling oysters by the side of the road since I was eight years old. I started pretty young. I quit school at around thirteen to

Tonging skiffs such as this one in Barataria Bay never had motors, but they were towed by a larger motorized vessel if travel was to be for any distance, 1945. (Courtesy Jean Landry)

Wilbert holding a pet raccoon (far right) with his father Levi Collins Jr., sister Tammy, and mother Betty, 1942. (Courtesy Wilbert Collins)

work full time on Dad's boat at $5 a day. Dredges came in, in 1951, right after I left school.

"My grandfather was opposed to dredges. He said that it would ruin the reefs—but it made them better. My father told me that the more you work a reef, the better. It unburies shells and the spats take better on reefs in growing areas. On planting reefs, like near Grand Isle, oyster spat didn't set, but working reefs makes them harder."

Levi Jr. worked until he was seventy-three, when a heart attack side-lined him. He lived twelve more years. Wilbert got married in 1954 while still working on his father's boat. "I got $10 dollars a day then," he says in half-amusement. "In some years I would bring home only $1,500 in the whole year."

In the 1970s, Wilbert says that he began taking more interest in the business and doing more. The take-over from his father was gradual. "Dad was always the captain and I was always the deck hand." In 1964, the elder Collins built a second boat and both men became captains. But the oyster market still wasn't that good. They sold some oysters to shucking houses, some to steam factories, and sent some to western Louisiana for retail sale. Markets in Abbeville, New Iberia, and Lafayette would take five hundred sacks a week.

The decks-awash, **Capt. Wilbert** *is loaded with seed oysters during the 1985 bumper year. (Courtesy Wilbert Collins)*

Hand gathering of oysters, called "cooning," is an old but still-practiced method of harvesting oysters. (Courtesy Brian Gauvin, Gauvin Photography)

In the 1960s, Collins says, the oyster fishery was mostly in the wintertime. Only one truck would buy thirty sacks a week in the summer for delivery. In the summer, the men moved oysters, got boats ready, and marked leases, and in May they trapped snails, which are strong oyster predators. "In May, people stopped eating oysters," he explains. "The oysters got milky then and people didn't like eating them. We started planting seed oysters from our own leases in August and from the state seed grounds in September. We started selling to the public in November.

"On Bayou Lafourche, we had sixteen family oyster companies, with three or four boats apiece that would plant oysters for three or four months. Today, I am the only one left with three boats. There are a few little boats left with people that fish oysters by hand [cooning]. The old people died and their kids took it over a while and then sold out."

Numbers bear out the historical contribution of Cajun oystermen. A 1902 Department of Conservation survey of the number of oyster leases and ownership by ethnic surname showed that 28 percent of all leases statewide were held by French-surnamed owners, compared to 12 percent by "Slavonians," as Croatians were referred to then. The largest group by surname were English (34 percent), but this approach likely under-counted the French, because many Cajuns, like the Collinses, had English surnames due to intermarriage.

He goes on, "Each of those families would plant as much as one hundred loads [of seed oysters] a year—mostly for steam. We had three steam factories on Bayou Lafourche. But the lack of oysters caused the steam factories to close. There just wasn't enough seed for people to plant. The sack business got great and sack fishermen fished them out of the seed grounds. Came a time they were sacking everything.

"Millions and million of cans, they used to can. Now they are all gone. Prices went up to $24 a sack in the late 1980s and 1990. Then, we had a big crop and by '92, oysters fell to $8.

"Since [Hurricane] Katrina, I didn't have enough oysters for my business. Before Katrina, we would sell thousands of sacks a year. People would drive a long way—Opelousas, even Shreveport—six to ten thousand sacks a year. Just Christmas week I would sell a thousand sacks.

"Katrina stopped our planting and disrupted business. We didn't have oysters to plant from areas across the river—Black Bay seed ground. Then fresh water destroyed my crops on my leases. Since BP, we have lost a lot of money. I lost seven crops in the spill. Eighty

Wilbert Collins' oyster sign was for decades as much of a fixture as nearby Dufrene's Bakery on Highway 1 in Golden Meadow.

percent of my farm was destroyed—nine hundred acres completely lost—100 percent."

He pauses, seemingly lost in thought. "I remember Hurricane Betsy in 1965. We were getting seed oysters across the [Mississippi] river when we heard the news. We tried to come home but so many people were leaving by car, they wouldn't open the Empire Bridge to let boats pass.

"Finally they let us cross and we went through the locks into Grand Lake [Barataria Bay]. The storm was moving fast. It was coming at twenty miles an hour and we could only travel six miles per hour. It hit us in Grand Lake.

"The water all went out of the lake. It was just mud where it was normally four or five feet deep. When it got really bad, we tied all three Collins boats together. The wind got so strong it was throwing mud from the bottom of the lake on the boats. It was plastered everywhere—plastered in cracks, plastered inside the cabin. The tents [awnings]: it tore that up like it was nothing.

"Then the wind switched. When it shifted, within seconds the water came—a seven-foot wave. We had no control of nothing. In seconds the boats were separated and nobody had untied a rope.

"We were all on the big boat, the sixty-foot *Capt. Wilbert.* The *Wilbert Jean,* [a fifty-two-footer] blew toward Lafitte. We found it and recovered it. The little boat, a forty-foot boat with no name—we never found it.

"I never really got scared, but you have to go through it to see what a storm can do in a little while. It all took place at night. One thing that I regret was after we picked up the *Wilbert Jean,* there was a dog swimming. We never picked it up. I always kept that in my mind— that poor dog—he was a black Labrador. Only thing I can figure, he came ten, fifteen miles from Grand Isle. There was a lot of debris in the water from camps on Grand Isle.

"From there, we traveled to Grand Isle and passed through Caminada Bay in East Canal to Leeville. Power lines were sagging in the water there. We met up with five other oyster boats that were caught out. They were scared to pass the power lines—scared they might catch them in their wheel [propeller] and scared if they were live.

"Finally, I said to Roger Toups to come on the *Wilbert Jean* and throw the anchor over the wires. 'I can do that' he said. He threw the anchor and I backed the boat up and broke the lines.

"We got home and there was a lot of damage. All the telephone posts were down. A week later we went back across the river to plant. Homes were still without power and we didn't have light plants [generators] in those days. My daughter was born two days after I got home. Two days later I left my wife and the baby to go on the boat.

"I have no regrets. I worked hard. I worked in storms. I worked in northwesters. I worked in sleet. I worked in snow—but we did it. My father was strict. When we had an order, we had to do it. I kept on like that even after Daddy was gone."

A Walk Through an Oyster-Shucking House

With the notable exception of oysters shucked in hydrostatic high pressure systems, most oysters are still shucked completely by hand, the way the Romans did it two thousand years ago. Oysters are living creatures when they meet the knife in the shucking stall and stubbornly resist being removed from their shells. Hand shucking demands skill and dexterity. Although most oysters shucked in shucking houses will be cooked before being eaten, a few will be consumed raw, so all of them are handled quickly and sanitarily and kept as cold as possible. A walk through the P&J Oyster Company shucking house in New Orleans provides a look at how shucked oysters are produced.

Company-owned refrigerated trucks pick up oysters in sacks directly from harvesters in Empire and Port Sulphur for delivery to the plant.

The palletized oysters are removed from the truck by a fork lift and moved with a pallet jack into a walk-in cooler set at 38 degrees Fahrenheit.

When oysters are needed for shucking, a pallet jack is used to retrieve them from the cooler and a fork lift is used to lift them to the shuckers' stalls, where they are emptied by the fork lift operator, one sack at a time, per stall.

Shuckers sanitize and cool their stainless-steel buckets before starting by washing them with soapy water, rinsing with a bleach solution, and then adding a quart of water and a quart of ice to each bucket.

Each oyster is handled and opened individually and carefully to avoid tearing its tender flesh. Oysters are shucked directly into the buckets.

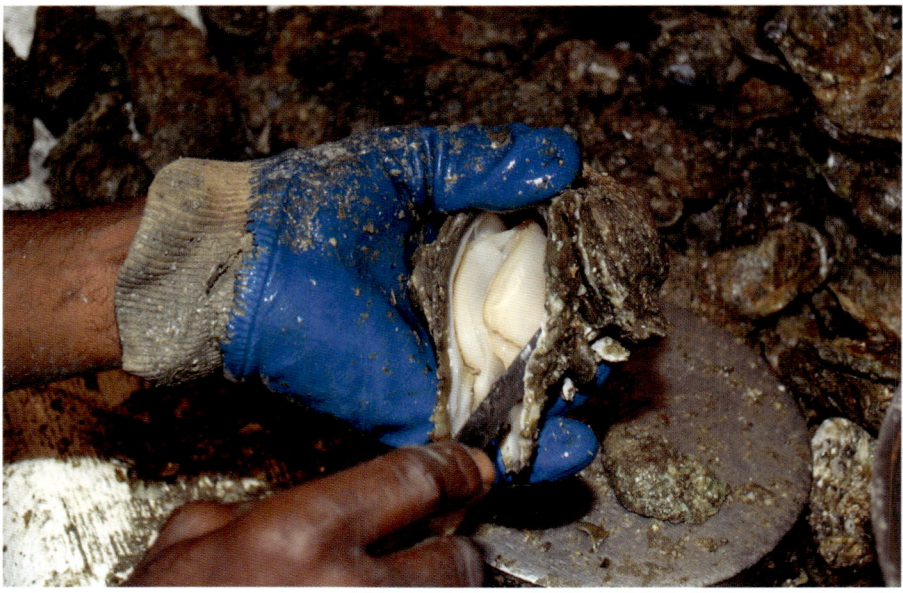

Shuckers drop empty shells through holes in their bins to the floor beneath the bins. The empty shells will be removed at the end of the shift.

After finishing a sack, a shucker takes the pail to the packing room to exchange it for a clean one. In the packing room, the oysters are emptied from the pail into a large, stainless-steel bowl and flushed with water so that shell particles fall to the bottom. The oysters are gently moved from the bowl onto a perforated skimming table, rinsed, and then put into plastic containers for weighing to determine yield-per-sack.

The oysters are emptied into a large, stainless-steel blowing tank held near 32 degrees with ice. Air is fed into the bottom of the tank through a perforated tube for five minutes. The air bubbles churn the water and oysters and create foam, which is regularly skimmed off the surface. More freshwater is introduced into the tank to further clean the oysters.

The oysters are drained from the blowing tank to the skimming table, stirred to allow any remaining shell particles to settle through the perforations in the table, and then drained.

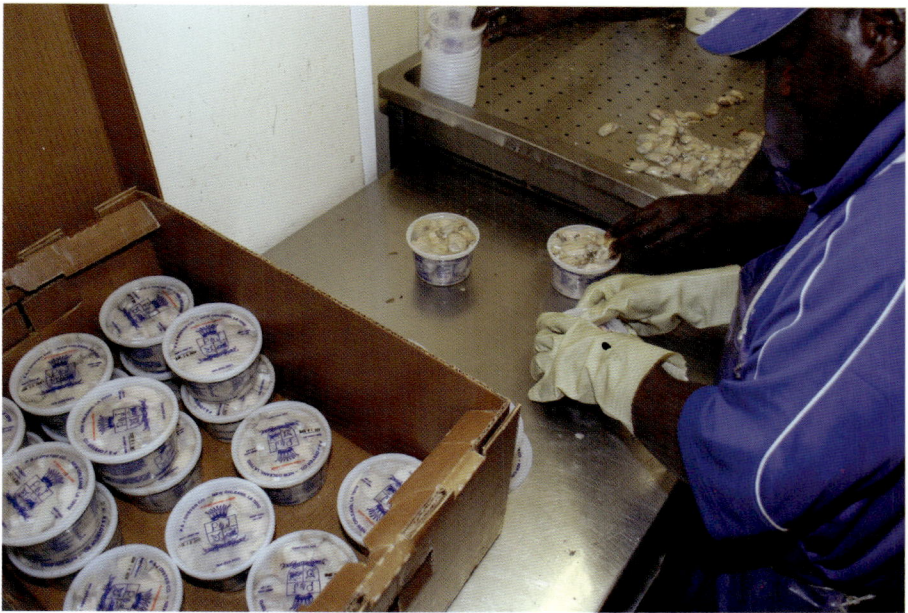

After draining, the oysters are hand-packed to order into various-sized containers, and the containers are placed in waxed cardboard boxes.

The shucked and packed oysters are buried in ice and moved to a second cooler, held just above freezing.

Shortly before sale, the oysters are unpacked and checked for weight loss. More oysters are added, if necessary. They are repacked in ice for delivery by refrigerated truck.

Creating a More Perfect Oyster

Dr. John Supan, LSU research professor and Louisiana's unofficial oyster ambassador, will be quick to tell anyone that the best oysters in the United States come from Louisiana's fertile waters. But that hasn't stopped him from trying to make the best better.

The oyster found in Louisiana is officially called the eastern oyster: the same species that is found in the other Gulf states and up the Atlantic Coast. Eastern oysters follow a predictable annual cycle. All winter they feed almost non-stop, growing plump with stored energy reserves. These are the oysters revered by ostraphiles; the ones they call "fat oysters."

Then with the onset of warm temperatures in spring they begin to spawn. They spawn, and they spawn, and then they spawn some more. Veritable sex machines, they so give their lives over to producing eggs and sperm that they burn up and use all their stored energy or fat. By mid-summer, the oysters will be shriveled ghosts of their former selves, often weighing only one-third of what they did six months earlier. These are "skinny oysters."

Dr. John Supan is director of the LSU oyster hatchery research facility.

Although still safe to eat, they have lost much of their rich mouthfeel and have become flabby. Worse, oyster-shucking houses have to shuck three times as many oysters to make a gallon of oyster meats in summer than in the winter.

Supan is on a quest to produce a naturally non-spawning oyster, which, when combined with superior growing techniques, will grow faster and remain fat year-round. At first glance it seems impossible. Where will the next generation of oysters come from, if this generation doesn't reproduce?

His approach is to mess with the "ploidy" or number of chromosomes in their genetic make-up. Most animals are "diploid," meaning that they have two sets of chromosomes: one set from their male parent and the other set from the female parent.

"Triploid" oysters have three sets of chromosomes, which makes them sexually sterile. They are produced in a hatchery by crossing diploid female oysters with "tetraploid" oysters, which have four sets of chromosomes. Fertilized eggs were chemically tricked into tetraploidy to produce the first generation of tetraploids, which are fertile and breed true in normal spawning events thereafter. Supan

The oyster hatchery contains tanks of oysters that spawn busily all summer.

Triploid oysters, such as the one shown here, held by Supan in late July, remain plump and firm all through the summer.

and his colleagues have produced this special parent stock, which was first developed for Pacific and Atlantic Coast hatcheries, for use in the Gulf of Mexico.

Triploid oysters, Supan's production goal at the Louisiana Sea Grant Program's Oyster Hatchery at Grand Isle, have great potential as a new "summer crop" of oysters to switch to when normal diploid meat yields begin their usual, seasonal decline.

Tetraploid and triploid oysters are not "genetically modified organisms," as no gene-splicing is done. Polyploidy, the presence of more than the usual two chromosomes, is common in the natural plant world. Bananas and sugar beets are triploid, blueberries are tetraploid, and wheat is actually hexaploid, having six chromosomes.

Supan is also an advocate of growing high-value oysters in baskets suspended off the bottom by longlines, racks, rafts, or other floating culture systems. The experimental longline system at the oyster hatchery resembles nothing so much as a semi-submerged vineyard. On the bottom, it takes a minimum of two years for a tiny fingernail-size oyster to grow to harvestable size. Suspended off the bottom in baskets, the oysters are large enough to harvest in one year.

Supan has had excellent results growing out triploid oysters at the hatchery. Commercial culture of triploid oysters with off-bottom culture systems is the next step to providing fat oysters to the marketplace in the summertime.

One of the methods for cultivating superior triploid oysters that Supan has experimented with is baskets suspended off the water bottom on longlines.

The Oyster Life Cycle

Oysters are a "protandric" species, meaning that they all start life as males, with many changing sex to females later in life. In their first year, larger oysters are more likely than smaller oysters to change to females. The change seems to be heavily dependent on the food supply available. Food limitations lead to a greater number of males in the population. Females also need a good food supply to produce eggs in large numbers.

A single female can produce 10 to 20 million eggs per spawn, with occasional spawnings of 100 million. In one season, a female can produce as many as 500 million eggs. Spawning typically begins when water temperatures warm to 77 degrees Fahrenheit and continues until the fall. The eggs are released into the water and fertilized at random by sperm released by male oysters on the reef.

Within a couple of days of development, a veliger larva is produced from each fertilized egg that has survived. These swimming larvae use the hairs (cilia) on their shell to move in the water and to gather the single-celled algae on which they feed. In turn, huge numbers of veligers are eaten by predators. Currents sweep them far and wide. Too much or too little salt in the water will kill them. Only a few veligers make it to a suitable site.

The veligers seem to find hard surfaces by following a chemical trail or signal that some researchers believe is given off by a bacterial film that develops on the hard surfaces. Once the veliger receives the signal, it begins to change into a spat, which will cement itself to the hard surface and begin growing into a recognizable oyster. The best surface for spat to settle on is oyster shell, but spat will cement to almost any hard surface.

Besides diseases, oysters have many natural enemies. Oyster drills—snails with tube-shaped, rasp-like tongues—drill holes through the oysters' shells. Both blue crabs and stone crabs dine heavily on small oysters. Finfish eat oysters, too. Sheepshead will eat small oysters, and black drum will eat oysters of any size, being stymied only by oysters in big clusters.

With average Louisiana conditions, it takes at least two and usually three years for an oyster to reach marketable size. Because of predators (including humans) and diseases, oysters seldom live longer than five years.

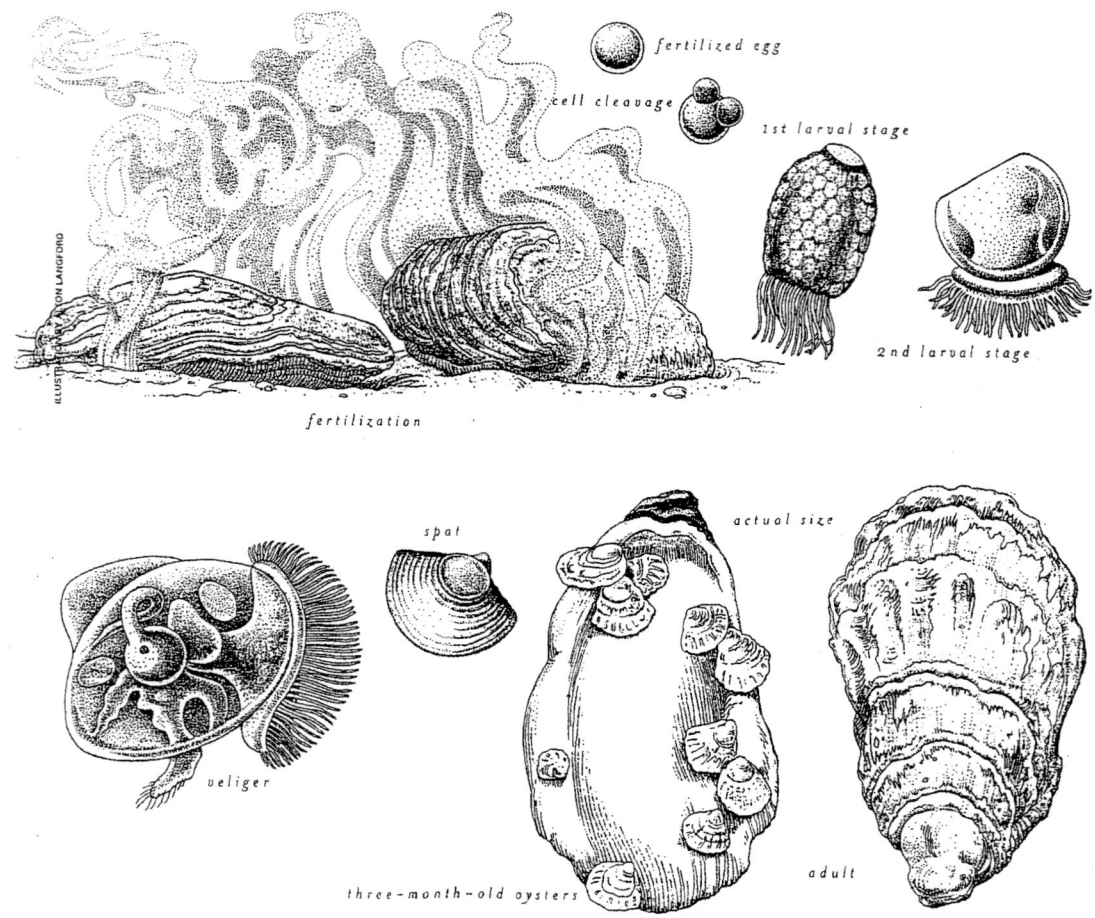

The oyster life cycle. (Courtesy Alton Langford)

Oyster reefs are incredibly important to the health of coastal lakes and bays, and in fact, oysters have been called the "keystone of inshore marine life." They are living pumps that feed by filtering microscopic phytoplankton (one-celled plants) from the water. One oyster can filter up to six gallons of water per hour. Oyster reefs are also prime fishing locations for recreational fishermen who pursue speckled trout and redfish. Finally, of course, the oysters are valuable to the oysterman whose living depends upon them and to the restaurants and markets that sell them. Oystermen try to maintain existing reefs and build new ones in the face of constant salinity changes and a seemingly endless number of oyster predators.

Alien Oysters

Louisianans are so proud of their oysters that just the thought of someone selling oysters in Louisiana, which hail from another place, is alien to them. But it does occur. For example, seasonal and yearly variations in price and supply will occasionally result in Texas oysters being sold in Louisiana.

Less common are shucked oysters from the state of Washington in Louisiana markets. Unlike Texas oysters, which are the same species of oyster as the Louisiana oyster, *Crassostrea virginica*, the Washington oyster is an entirely different species, *Crassostrea gigas*.

The taste differences between the two are dramatic, and a typical Louisiana oyster connoisseur would likely struggle with the taste of Pacific oysters. Pacific oysters can grow to impressively large sizes—as big as the sole of a man's size twelve shoe and nearly a pint in volume—although most are sold at smaller sizes. Pacific oysters are

Even very large Olympia oysters, such as these, are tiny by Louisiana standards.

usually labeled either as Pacific oysters or as Washington oysters, when sold here. They have a soapy, iodine taste.

An American oyster that even the best food sleuth (unfortunately) will not likely find in Louisiana or the Gulf South is the tiny Olympia oyster, *Ostrea lurida*. Taking from 2,000 to 2,500 meats to make a gallon, the tiny "Olys" are an epicurean delight, with their brilliant coppery tang and sea-salt finish. The very small Olympia harvest that occurs also comes from the state of Washington.

All three of these oysters are produced in the U.S. and country-of-origin labeling (COOL) rules allow these oysters to be sold as products of the U.S.A. COOL requirements for seafood were passed by Congress in 2002. Under the law, retailers, except for seafood specialty stores and restaurants, which are both exempt, must inform consumers by a clear label or sign what country the product is from and whether it is wild-caught or farm-raised.

A few imported oyster products do reach Louisiana. Canned oysters, once a major product of Louisiana, are now imported from Asia, primarily China and Korea. Frozen-on-the-half-shell oysters are also imported in small amounts from Korea.

For seafood to be labeled as a product of the U.S., farm-raised seafood must be hatched, raised, and processed in the U.S. Wild-caught seafood must be harvested from U.S. waters or by a U.S. flagged vessel and processed in the U.S.

Some exceptions from COOL regulations do exist. Cooked, cured, smoked, canned, or surimi-type products are exempt from labeling. When two or more different seafoods are mixed together they do not need to be labeled, even if they are all imports. Also exempt from labeling requirements are substantially modified seafoods such as breaded products, marinated products, soups, sauces, seafood salads, cocktails, sushi, and pâté.

Other Louisiana Mollusks

Louisianans eat lots of crustaceans—crabs, shrimp, and crawfish—but seldom eat more than one kind of mollusk and that one would be oysters. But other edible mollusks do exist in Louisiana. Mollusks, with the exception of one class, can be characterized by their very hard calcium carbonate shells. The world's 93,000 or so species can be broken into eight classes. Though all classes are edible, only three appeal to our palate and are found in Louisiana: bivalves (oysters, clams, scallops, and mussels), gastropods (snails and slugs), and cephalopods (octopus and squid).

Bivalves are named so because they have two valves or shells. Besides oysters, Louisiana has two other species of bivalves that some have attempted to commercialize. In the mid-to-late 1970s, the Pausina family of New Orleans made a private effort to develop a fishery for the large, southern quahog, *Mercenaria campechiensis.* The southern quahog is found in the Gulf of Mexico and is a close relative of the northern quahog of the Atlantic coast.

Southern quahogs grow to large sizes.

The northern quahog provides a large fishery for hard clams along the U.S. mid-to-north Atlantic coast. The northern quahog is marketed by size: 2 to 2½ inches are littlenecks, 2½ to 3 inches are topnecks, 3 to 4 inches are cherrystones, and larger than 4 inches are chowders. The larger the clam, the tougher the flesh is and the lower the price. Littlenecks are tender enough to be eaten raw, but they are often steamed as well. Chowders are so tough that they must be cooked to tenderize them.

Southern hard clams are similar to northern hard clams, but they have a slightly more pronounced taste. Several years of fishing effort in inshore waters east of the Mississippi River produced mostly cheaper, chowder-size clams. The fishery ceased after 1979.

Rangia clams, *Rangia cuneata*, are much smaller than quahogs and prefer substantially lower salinity waters. They are found in huge numbers and are so common that they were dredged to use in place of gravel on south Louisiana roads. However, their predilection for low-salinity waters means that they are most abundant in waters closed to shellfish harvesting because of proximity to civilization and pollution.

Indian tribes made extensive use of rangia, producing many shell

Rangia clams are one of the most common mollusks in Louisiana estuarine waters.

mounds or middens, where they discarded the empty shells of the creatures after liberating the flesh. Europeans made little use of these abundant clams because, though quite delicious raw, cooking produced unpleasant changes in the taste of the flesh.

In the 1980s, substantial federal funding was obtained to study the development of a fishery for these small clams, which are the same size as pricy north Atlantic littleneck hard clams. The clams were immediately dubbed "Cajun clams." Research focused on relaying the clams from polluted waters to clean, high-salinity waters and developing a processing technique which would prevent the formation of the musty flavors produced during cooking.

Relaying worked well, producing delicious clams, so long as they were eaten raw. The second part of the research failed to produce a satisfactory answer to the cooking taste-change and the infant commercial fishery disappeared.

Gastropods are by far the largest class of mollusks in the world. Louisiana has many marine snails, most or all of which are edible,

The flesh of an oyster drill is easy to remove from the shell after boiling a short while.

including relatively large welks. But the only one eaten with any frequency is the oyster drill, *Stramonita haemastoma.* Invariably known as "bigorneau" to Cajun oystermen or "conch" to Croatians, this is a highly predacious snail. They are the number one predator of oysters in high-salinity waters, using their rasp-like tongues to bore though oysters' shells and eat them alive.

They are frequently caught as bycatch by oyster fishermen and at times by crabbers as well. Many oystermen save and clean them; they freeze well. Cleaning is done by boiling them in the shell for a few minutes, until the meat is firm and easy to extract with a knife-tip or pick. To finish cleaning them, cut off the dark, inky viscera sack from the end of the creamy white meat. The word gastropod means "stomach-foot" in Latin and refers to the proximity of the viscera to the "foot" muscle. In fact, the extracted animal appears to be all viscera and foot. This tasty snail benefits from long cooking to tenderize it. They can often be obtained from oystermen by special request.

Cephalopod means "head-foot" in Latin and at first glance an octopus, one of the more familiar cephalopods, appears to be just that—a head with eight feet (arms) sticking out of it. Squid differ only in being streamlined and having two longer tentacles as well as eight arms. Both octopus and squid are found in Louisiana, but only squid are common enough to be considered as a food source. Three kinds of squid are found in or offshore of the state. Longfin squid (*Loligo*) are the largest, growing up to twenty-four inches long counting the

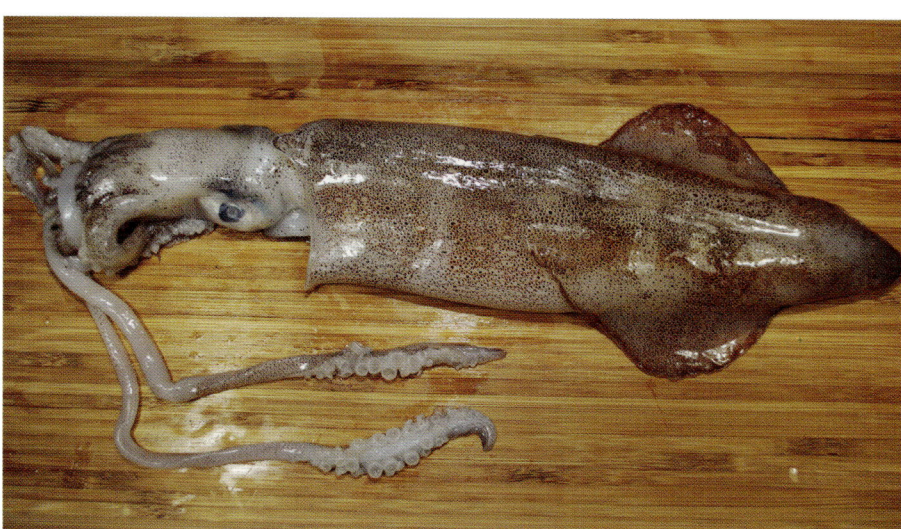

Longfin squid are the largest and easiest to clean of Louisiana's several squid species.

tentacles, and the easiest to clean. Shortfin squid *(Illex)* can grow to twelve inches. The tiny brief squid *(Lolliguncula)* seldom grows more than four inches long and is difficult to clean because of its size. It is, however, the most abundant Louisiana squid and the only one found in interior brackish lakes and bays.

Squid are very common bycatch in the shrimp fishery. Finfish excluders do not eject them. Shrimpers often cook them at sea or save them for friends, family, and others who request them. Squid freeze extremely well.

Oyster Product Forms Available

Oysters are available in a variety of product forms, including live sack oysters, live graded half-shell oysters in sacks or boxes, post-harvest processed half-shell oysters, individually quick frozen (IQF) half-shell oysters, fresh shucked oyster meats, and frozen shucked oyster meats.

Live sack oysters are typically sold in burlap sacks that hold 1½ bushels. Half-sacks are also available. The oysters in sacks and half-sacks are not graded to any uniform size or shape. However, live oysters graded to a size suitable for half-shell use are also sold. These oysters are usually packed in smaller sacks, sometimes called mini-sacks, or in waxed cardboard boxes. Graded oysters may be sold by count (one hundred to two hundred per container) or by volume or weight.

Post-harvest processed oysters (sometimes called post-harvest treated oysters) are typically destined for the half-shell trade, although many are also shucked. These oysters are graded for quality and size and then processed to reduce the levels of the bacterium *Vibrio*

"Box oysters" are graded for size and quality and are destined for raw oyster bars.

vulnificus, as well as other *Vibrio* bacteria, to non-detectable levels. Post-harvest processed half-shell oysters are sold by count and packed in waxed boxes.

IQF half-shell oysters are simply oysters that have been opened and then quickly frozen at very cold temperatures on one half of their shell. The very cold temperatures used minimize undesirable textural changes caused by freezing. They are typically sold twelve dozen per waxed cardboard box.

Fresh-shucked oyster meats can be purchased in gallon, half-gallon, quart, pint, and eight-ounce containers. Occasionally, ten and twelve-ounce containers are also available. They may also be sold by count, especially in retail seafood specialty stores. For shucked oysters, Louisiana law allows up to 15 percent free liquid by weight in any container sold by weight or volume. Frozen shucked oysters are usually sold by weight and are most often packed in heavy, sealed poly bags.

In Louisiana, oysters sold by the gallon are packed "straight run," meaning that they are not graded by size. Some shucking houses will grade oysters, primarily for the Atlantic Coast market, into "selects" and "standards." Standards are forty to eighty per pound of shucked meats; selects are twenty five to thirty per pound. Shucked oysters graded to size must be specially ordered.

Contrary to popular belief, it is legal for oyster shucking houses to sell both containers of oyster liquor and unwashed oysters. Oyster liquor is simply the flavorful liquid left in the container that oysters were shucked into, after the oysters have been removed from it.

A full sack of oysters is quite a burden, even for a strong man like Mitch Jurisich, Jr.

Shucked oysters can be found in various size containers, which are usually plastic but occasionally glass, as well.

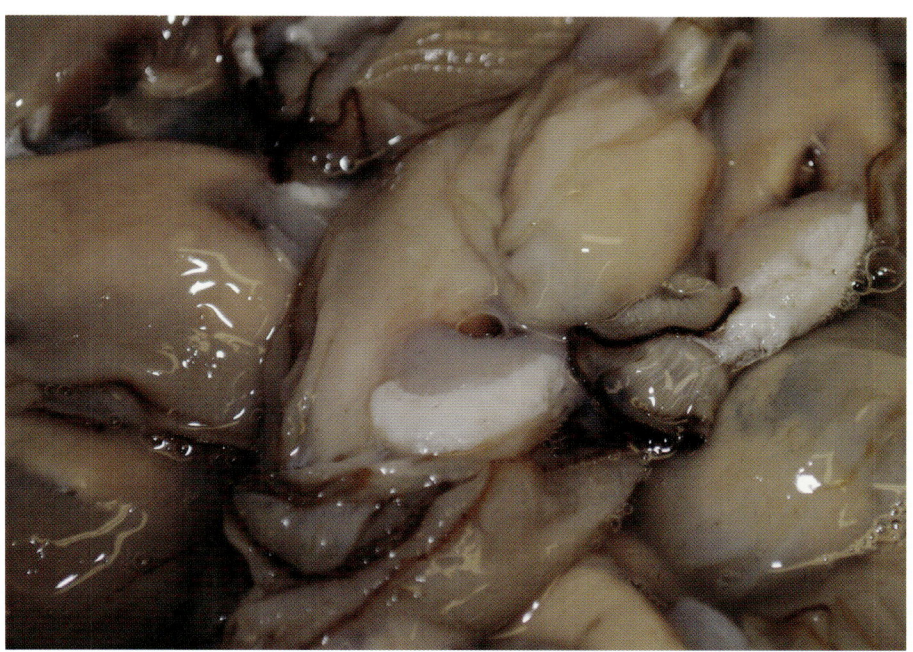

Louisiana shucking houses usually produce straight run oysters.

Oyster shucking houses wash their oysters in fresh water as a standard practice to improve the appearance of the oyster meats and, most importantly, to get rid of any stray shell pieces. Washing, however, does wash away some of the salty flavor so loved by many oyster aficionados.

Most wholesale shucking houses will reserve unwashed oysters and even oyster liquor by special request. So will seafood retail specialty stores that hold the appropriate licenses permitting them to shuck oysters.

Purchasing oysters can be confusing and leave retail buyers perplexed about how many oysters to buy to prepare a recipe. The rules don't seem like the rules. For example, many people assume that a gallon of oysters contains eight pounds of shucked meats. After all, a gallon holds 8 pints and "a pint is a pound the whole world round." They are utterly dismayed when they bring home their purchase and find their gallon container holds only five or even four pints (pounds) of oysters.

The problem arises because in the wholesale trade, oysters are bought and sold by the pound, but packed in gallon or half-gallon plastic containers. Terms such as five-pound gallons, seven-pound gallons, or solid packs (eight-pound gallons) are common within the

A solid pack of oysters is completely full.

trade. Unfortunately, usually for competitive pricing reasons, gallon containers that hold less than a consumer might expect will work their way into the retail trade.

Most consumers quickly assume that they have been cheated. Usually, but not always, they haven't. Typically, they price-shopped and bought the cheapest "gallon" they could find. And most likely, it was the cheapest because it had fewer pounds of shucked meats in it. This is a common occurrence.

An individual buying gallons or even half-gallons of oysters at the retail level should, as a matter of routine, always ask how many pounds of oyster meats are in the container. The seller will know. If he or she doesn't, the seller is being evasive for a reason and it is best to make the purchase elsewhere. Dividing the pounds of meat in the gallon into the price provides much more accurate price information than does purchasing by volume.

Further confusion arises because some recipes call for a pint of oysters, while others call for a pint of drained oysters or a pint of shucked oysters. These are different. Oysters routinely lose some liquids from within their bodies after being packed in their retail containers. Weights and measures laws recognize that as a fact. Consumers should not expect sixteen ounces of oysters in a pint container, but rather twelve to fourteen ounces. Quarts will contain twenty-four to twenty-eight ounces of meats and an eight-ounce container will hold six to seven ounces.

Finally, many recipes call for oysters by number, for example twenty-four or thirty-six. Although straight-run packed Louisiana oysters vary somewhat in size, thirty to forty oysters will be in a pint container, averaging about thirty-five per container.

Harvesting the Oyster

Because oysters and some other molluscan shellfish are filter feeders and are eaten raw, special efforts are made to protect public health. U.S. coastal waters are surveyed according to guidelines provided by the National Shellfish Sanitation Program. The surveys cover 4,230 shellfish growing areas in twenty-one coastal states. These areas are put into one of five categories.

- Approved. Shellfish from these areas may be harvested for direct marketing, unless the area is specially closed for some reason.
- Conditionally Approved. These are shellfish-growing waters that meet the Approved classification under predictable conditions, such as with seasonal changes in river flows.
- Restricted. Shellfish may only be harvested from these waters if they are relayed or depurated before marketing.
- Conditionally Restricted. These waters do not meet the restricted classification if they have off-and-on bacterial pollution, but the shellfish may be harvested if they are put through a suitable purification process.
- Prohibited. No shellfish harvest is allowed from these waters.

Shellfish-growing water quality has improved dramatically in the U.S. Between 1974 and 1995, the number of acres in the Approved classification has increased by more than 40 percent. The acreage in the Conditionally Approved and Restricted classifications has also increased and the acreage classified as Prohibited has declined.

Bad Bugs and Oysters

I have long believed that good food, good eating is all about risk. Whether we are eating unpasteurized Stilton, raw oysters, or working for organized crime "associates," food for me, has always been an adventure.
— Anthony Bourdain (b 1956),
American chef, author, and television personality

To many people a fat, salty, raw oyster on the half-shell is heaven. Oysters are filter-feeders, who live by straining microscopic one-celled plants called phytoplankton from the sea's waters. One oyster can filter up to six gallons of water in an hour.

Unfortunately, they also occasionally filter out a "bad bug," a virus or a bacterium that can cause illness in a person who eats the oyster raw. Eating raw oysters (and clams) is an important culinary activity for seafood connoisseurs, and oyster culture and harvest for the raw market is important for coastal economies.

Raw shellfish are so important that the U.S. Food and Drug Administration (FDA) and coastal state governments oversee the National Shellfish Sanitation Program, which sets standards for waters in which shellfish are grown and requires those waters to be tested regularly. The program is designed to ensure that shellfish are harvested from certified waters and meet safety standards. Because of this program, large amounts of raw clams and oysters are eaten each year with few incidents of illness.

In spite of the efficiency of the program, some risks, especially for some people, exist in the consumption of raw oysters and clams. The risks come from both viruses and bacteria. Virus outbreaks, which are rare because of tight controls and monitoring within the shellfish sanitation program, most often involve the Norwalk virus or Hepatitis A virus.

The Norwalk virus causes short-term gastroenteritis, commonly resulting in nausea, cramps, vomiting, and diarrhea. Symptoms begin twenty-four to forty-eight hours after contaminated food or water is consumed, and last twenty-four to sixty hours. It is usually written off as a "stomach bug" and typically dehydration is the only serious health concern. Norwalk and Norwalk-like viruses have also been associated with non-oyster-related outbreaks of illness on cruise ships, in communities, camps, schools, institutions, and families. Besides oysters, foods such as cake frosting and salads, as well as drinking water, have been implicated as a common source of viral infection in outbreaks.

Illness from Hepatitis A is much less common. Hepatitis A is less serious than Hepatitis B or C and does not usually cause long-term illness nor organ damage. Symptoms include tiredness, fever, loss of appetite, and abdominal discomfort. Mild cases are often dismissed as the flu. In more serious cases, jaundice and darkening of the urine may occur and medical attention may be necessary. Once a person is infected with Hepatitis A, he or she will have immunity to further such infections for life.

For a few people, the naturally occurring bacterium, *Vibrio vulnificus*, is more serious than viruses. *V. vulnificus* are free-living organisms in warm brackish and marine waters and are in no way related to pollution. They are much more common in the warmer months of the year, when filter-feeding oysters can accumulate them in their bodies.

For most people, the presence of *V. vulnificus* in an oyster means nothing—nothing at all. But some people with pre-existing medical conditions are considered "at risk" for a severe blood infection (primary septicemia) or gastroenteritis. At-risk conditions include compromised immune systems, AIDS, cancer (especially during chemotherapy), liver disease, diabetes, hemochromatosis, chronic kidney disease, inflammatory bowel disease, steroid dependency, achlorhydria, and other stomach problems. Alcoholics and people on antacid therapy are also considered to be at-risk.

Primary septicemia occurs after food containing *V. vulnificus* is consumed and the bacteria invade the bloodstream via the digestive tract. The illness is characterized by fever and chills and is usually accompanied by nausea, vomiting, and diarrhea. A sharp drop in blood pressure commonly occurs, with the possible outcome of intractable shock and death. The majority of patients also develop painful skin lesions. The skin initially appears red; blisters develop quickly and then erode into necrotic ulcers.

Gastroenteritis occurs after ingesting food containing *V. vulnificus.* Patients with gastroenteritis have a somewhat milder syndrome consisting of vomiting, diarrhea, and abdominal cramps. Patients with gastroenteritis may require hospitalization, but they rarely die.

V. vulnificus septicemic infections are serious, resulting in death for 46 percent of the people who contract them. Prompt treatment is critical, because in fatal cases, the average time between hospital admission and death is forty-eight hours.

At-risk individuals can also be infected with *V. vulnificus* through wounds, cuts, punctures, or burns if they swim or wade in seawater. At-risk individuals should not clean or handle raw seafood without protection. Wound infections typically begin with swelling, redness, and intense pain around the infected site. Fluid-filled blisters often develop and progress to tissue necrosis in a rapid and severe process resembling gas gangrene. Fifty percent of patients with *V. vulnificus*-infected wounds require surgical tissue removal or amputation. In some patients, infection spreads to the bloodstream, and in such cases death commonly occurs.

At-risk individuals can eat oysters. Well-cooked (to an internal temperature of 140 degrees F) oysters are perfectly safe. The Interstate Shellfish Sanitation Commission also instructs that oysters that have had "post-harvest processing" (PHP) and are labeled "Processed to reduce *Vibrio vulnificus* to non-detectable levels" are also safe for at-risk people to consume. These oysters are close to indistinguishable from raw oysters and are even sold inside their original shells.

An excellent reference on seafood pathogens and parasites is the "Bad Bug Book" published by the U.S. Food and Drug Administration, available on their Web site.

Post-Harvest Processing
of Oysters

Vibrio vulnificus, a free-living, naturally occurring bacterium not associated with pollution, is changing the way half-shell oysters from the Gulf States are eaten. *V. vulnificus* is common in these waters during the warmer months, and filter-feeding shellfish such as oysters and clams can accumulate *V. vulnificus* as they feed.

When oysters with the bacterium are eaten by "at-risk" people who have pre-existing medical conditions, the bacteria can invade the bloodstream, resulting in serious illness and in almost half of the cases, death. Only a small percentage of the human population is considered high-risk, including those with liver disorders, such as hepatitis, cirrhosis, and liver cancer; hemochromatosis; diabetes mellitus; and those with immunocompromising conditions, such as HIV/AIDS, cancer, or those undergoing certain treatments. Individuals who take prescribed medication to decrease stomach acid levels or who have had gastric surgery are also at risk.

Although the number of deaths from *V. vulnificus* septicemia is very low, the publicity has been high. The U.S. Food and Drug Administration (FDA) seems bent on prohibiting the sale of Gulf States oysters for half-shell consumption during the warmer months of the year, unless the oysters have been post-harvest processed (PHP). Even without FDA strictures, some demand exists from healthy, but health-conscious consumers for PHP oysters, simply for peace of mind—to play it safe.

PHP subjects oysters to a treatment method that reduces *V. vulnificus* to non-detectable levels. All PHP treatment methods must be approved by the FDA before oysters can be labeled "Processed to reduce *Vibrio vulnificus* to non-detectable levels." Such oysters are safe for even at-risk people to eat.

The *V. vulnificus* bacterium, for being as virulent as it is to at-risk people, is surprisingly easy to kill. Currently, four PHP methods exist: hydrostatic high pressurization, low heat pasteurization, individual quick freezing (IQF), and irradiation. Only the first three processes are now being done on a commercial scale, although irradiation is on the cusp of practice.

In hydrostatic, high-pressure PHP, the oysters are placed in a steel cylinder filled with water and high pressures are applied with pumps. The process not only kills *Vibrio,* but it causes the oyster to "self-shuck." This process is patented. Hydrostatic, high-pressure-processed half-shell oysters are sold shrink-wrap-banded in their shells.

With low-heat pasteurization, also called heat-cool pasteurization, each oyster is individually banded with a rubber band, then placed in a precisely controlled warm water bath. This is followed by a shock bath in ice-cold water to further shock the bacteria and reduce heat in the oysters. This process is also patented.

Individually quick frozen oysters are frozen cryogenically. Some textural changes do occur, but IQF oysters have a shelf life of up to a year.

Irradiation involves exposing the oysters to doses of energy through gamma rays, electron beams, or x-rays. No irradiation method leaves behind any radiation or dangerous substances. In fact, if low doses are used in the process, the oyster is still alive after treatment. The drawback of irradiation is its cost and the instinctive, but unwarranted, fear of the process by American consumers.

Complete information about all companies that provide PHP oysters and other shellfish in the United States can be found on the Web by searching for the FDA Interstate Certified Shellfish Shippers List.

Gold Band oysters can be identified by the bright yellow-gold shrink-wrap band around each oyster.

AmeriPure oysters are individually banded with a rubber band bearing the company name.

Recognizing Quality in Oysters

Oysters are generally purchased either as live shell-stock or as fresh-shucked product. Live oysters are relatively simple to judge for freshness. Their shells should be firmly closed and not gapped open. If a gapped oyster closes its shell when it is tapped with an oyster knife, it is fine. If it doesn't, it is dead and fit only to be discarded.

The gap between the shells is often quite small and difficult to see; however, a gapped oyster makes a very easy-to-recognize hollow sound when the shell is tapped by an oyster knife or when two oysters are tapped together. The sound produced by tapping a live oyster is similar to that produced by tapping a rock.

Purchasers should always ask the seller if they may inspect the oysters before purchase. If the oysters at the top of the sack are fine,

A sure-fire method of checking live oysters is to tap the shell with the knife. If it rings hollow, the oyster should be discarded.

they all will be. If raw taste is a consideration in the purchase, this is the time to ask the seller to open one for a sample. This request is expected from an oyster connoisseur and refusal to allow a sampling may indicate that the oysters are skinny or not salty.

When purchasing live oysters, make sure the sack is tagged with a Louisiana Department of Wildlife and Fisheries tag. The tag is your assurance that the oysters were harvested from approved shellfish-growing waters and are traceable in the event of a problem.

Shucked-oyster quality is much more difficult to assess. The liquid in the container should be clear rather than cloudy. Oysters in containers should always be sold buried in ice. Avoid purchasing shucked oysters in containers that are simply displayed on a refrigerated shelf.

Louisiana law allows for up to 15 percent free liquid by weight for any shucked oysters sold by volume or weight. This is relatively easy to visually assess in the transparent containers used to sell pints or less. However, it is not easy to see in gallons and half gallons, which are usually packed in opaque, white, plastic containers. Ask your supplier for the weight of the oyster meats in the container. They know, so any attempt to evade giving an answer usually indicates short packaging weights.

Never purchase oysters in untagged sacks.

Some's Better 'n Others

Oysters vary in taste and quality more than any other Louisiana seafood. The difference between a fat, salty oyster from a prime location and a skinny, sweet oyster from a marginal location is hard to describe in words.

The words "fat" and "skinny" are often heard in discussions between oyster lovers. There are definite seasonal differences, and they are based on the oysters' life cycle. Skinny oysters are those that have used up their fat (glycogen) reserves in producing millions of eggs or sperm during the summer. The onset of spawning can vary by more than a month from one spot in Louisiana to another, but typically it begins in April.

A female oyster will produce 15 to 114 million eggs per spawn and up to 500 million before cooler fall temperatures bring spawning to a halt. By this time, both male and female oysters are skinny, shriveled ghosts of what they were in March.

The flabby, weakened oysters then devote the time from September to April to feeding and rebuilding their glycogen reserves. Oyster fat, or glycogen as it is properly called, is not really an animal fat, but a

The skinny oyster on the right is a shrunken ghost of the fat oyster on the left.

form of animal starch that serves as an energy source for the oyster. Fat oysters are strongly preferred, especially for raw consumption, and are at their best from some point in December to well into May. Fat oysters are creamy-white and opaque. Skinny oysters are gray in color and translucent.

The salt content in oysters is determined by the salinity of the water the oysters live in. Louisiana oysters vary considerably in salt content. In years of high river discharges or rainfall, oysters may be quite sweet (unsalty) in taste, especially in spring. The rest of the year they are salty, as they are year-round in years with low river discharges or rainfall. Because oysters are fattest in early spring, finding oysters for raw consumption that are fat and salty at the same time can be tricky in some years. Dedicated oyster lovers always manage to do it though.

That Louisiana oysters vary considerably in taste and size was recognized as early as 1758 by the French explorer, Antoine Simon Le Page du Pratz from his time in the colony between 1718 and 1734:

Near the lake, when we pass by the outlets to the sea, and continue along the coast, we meet with small oysters in great abundance, that are well tasted. On the other hand, when we quit the lake by another lake that communicates with one of the mouths of the river we meet with oysters four or five inches broad, and six or seven inches long. These large oysters eat best fried, having hardly any saltiness, but in other respects are large and delicate.

Finally, there is the subject of *terroir* (pronounced tare-WAHR), a French word for the taste of a place in food, definable in water, soils, and climate. Originally used in describing wine, coffee, and tea, the term has been expanded to include other foods, including seafood. *Terroir* embraces the concept that foods from specific areas have

Raw oyster lovers will eat them for breakfast.

specific "personalities" because of where they originate. Washington fishermen have capitalized on the concept with their Lummi Island salmon.

Oysters from different bays taste very different from each other. Taste varies even from one reef to another in the same bay system. In the heyday of New Orleans oyster consumption in the nineteenth century and the first half of the twentieth century, Louisiana oysters were often identified and purchased by place of origin. A detailed history of the Louisiana oyster industry is found in "The Development of the Louisiana Oyster Industry in the 19th Century," a PhD dissertation prepared by Louisiana State University graduate student Karen M. Wicker in 1979. The following excerpt from the dissertation shows how discriminating oyster connoisseurs describe just part of the variety of Louisiana oysters in the 1880s.

The finest oysters came from Four Bayous, Lake Peliot and Bayous Fontenelle, Cyrpian, Chalons and Cook. A slightly lower quality of oysters was produced in the Timbaliers, East Bay and the Great Lakes (Barataria Bay). These oysters commanded the highest price and constituted the majority of the raw shop and counter trade products reaching New Orleans through the French Market landings.

The Bayou Chalons oyster was described as being large, long and possessing a clean shell while those from Four Bayous were middling, round and firm. Oysters from Bayous Fontenelle and Cyprian were described as small, hard, and round, and much preferred by connoisseurs. Oysters from Lake Peliot were preferred for frying because they were round, very fat, and salty with a hard eye. Oysters from Bayou Cook were legendary for their flavor and most went to retail counters in New Orleans. They commanded a price of from $2.50 to $4.00 per barrel in the 1880s.

Oysters coming from the Timbalier grounds were clumped and long, while Salinas oysters were considered less rich in flavor than those of the highest quality. East Bay oysters were said to be of a very good kind, with a light-colored shell and very white inside and those from the Great Lakes were in demand because of their peculiar flavor. One account ranked the oysters from Grand Isle and Barataria Bay as being next to those from Bayou Cook in quality, but commanding about the same price as those from the Salinas (Salt Works Canal). In 1880, this amounted to $1.25 to $3.00 per barrel.

Today, oysters from all over Louisiana are just sold as "Louisiana oysters." But cognoscenti recognize that the taste differences remain.

Another variation, which seems to affect taste little, is the color of the oyster meat. Most notably, oyster meats may be tinged or entirely colored brown, reddish-brown, or black. These are often referred to as "cock oysters" in Louisiana and Mississippi. Most "old-timers" explain that these oysters are males and taste better. Cock oysters are usually smaller oysters.

The technical explanation for the dark colors is that they are due to the presence of metals, such as iron or copper. Metals are accumulated and discarded by special cells in the oysters' mantles.

Some oyster meats are attractively colored in darker hues.

Storing Oysters

Shucked and live oysters must be stored differently, because live oysters will die if stored at the same low temperatures that are appropriate for shucked oysters. Containers of shucked oysters should never be stored at temperatures above 38 degrees F and preferably as close to 32 degrees as possible.

Because home refrigerators would be too cold for other foods if set at 32 degrees, the ideal way to store shucked oysters is to put the container of oysters in ice in a large bowl and put the entire thing in the fridge. At refrigerator temperatures, the ice will melt very slowly and the oysters will be kept near freezing temperatures, but not frozen.

Live oysters are more difficult to store. Ideally they should be kept under refrigeration at 40 to 45 degree temperatures from the time of purchase until they are shucked. This both keeps the oysters alive longer and inhibits the growth of bacteria, such as *Vibrio vulnificus* and *Vibrio parahaemolyticus.*

Few people have a walk-in cooler or extra refrigerator at home, so most must store live oysters in an ice chest, on top of the ice. After a

Live oysters stored on ice should not have ice heaped over the top of the sack, because the melting ice water will dilute their briny taste.

substantial bed of ice is laid in the chest, layers of burlap (such as the sack they came in) or wet newspapers should be put on top of the ice.

Only then are the oysters put in the ice chest. If the oysters are placed in direct contact with the ice, they will die sooner than they should. Ice should not be put on top of the oysters, because its melt-water will dilute the salty taste of the oysters as it trickles over the shells and is taken up by the oyster.

The drain plug on the ice chest should be opened, both to allow melt-water to escape and to allow some air to enter the chest. Ideally, the ice chest should be stored in a shady spot, where it gets maximum protection from the sun's rays during the hottest part of the day, and in a location where the melt-water will not make a mess.

Freshly harvested live oysters should last a week, with proper storage. Shucked oysters held embedded in ice have a shelf life of two weeks after shucking.

Freezing and Thawing Oysters

Oysters are not commonly thought of as a seafood item suitable for freezing. Can oysters be frozen at home? The answer is a qualified yes, but you must expect some changes to the oysters.

The frozen oyster will never taste like a freshly shucked oyster on the half-shell. There will be changes in flavor and texture, as well as drip loss during thawing. Drip loss is simply loss of some of the moisture from inside the cells of the oyster. This occurs when ice crystals pop the cells, letting the juices escape.

Frozen oysters are good for frying and excellent for use in gumbos and soups. The important thing to remember is to use good, live oysters and freeze them very rapidly in a cold freezer. It is also better to freeze them in pint containers, rather than quarts, because they will freeze faster. The faster they freeze, the less drip loss will occur and the firmer the texture will be.

To freeze oysters, shuck them into a strainer and save the clear liquor. Wash the oysters and after putting them in the freezing container, top it with the liquor. Add water if it's needed to cover the oysters.

Another neat way of freezing oysters is to freeze them in plastic ice trays, putting one oyster in each cavity of the tray. When they are

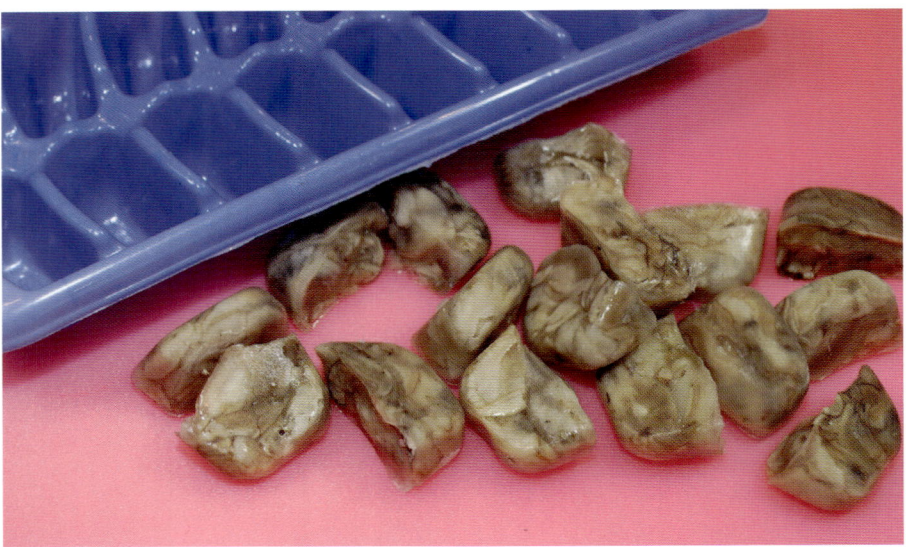

Freezing oysters in ice trays is easy to do and makes them quick to thaw and very convenient to use.

frozen, pop them out and store them in a heavy duty freezer bag or a plastic container.

This method has a couple of advantages. First, the oysters freeze much quicker than if they are in a pint container. Faster freezing means smaller ice crystals, less cell damage, and, therefore, reduced drip loss. Also, you can thaw out and use exactly as many oysters as you need, rather than having to thaw out a whole container.

Some research has shown that steaming oysters for fifteen minutes before shucking makes them not only easier to open, but also stops or slows down some of the changes that occur when they are frozen. Steamed frozen oysters have been shown to be acceptable for as long as six months if dipped in 1 percent ascorbic acid before freezing. You can do the same thing by dipping them in lemon juice diluted with water.

Oysters on the half shell are frozen by seafood processors, but these are individually quick frozen at temperatures far below what can be achieved in home freezers. Some oysters are also commercially frozen in polyethylene bags.

Oysters are very soft-fleshed and may experience some tissue damage when frozen. During thawing, the fluids from the damaged tissues will drain off as drip loss or thaw loss. One way to reduce drip loss is simply to drop the still-frozen oysters directly into a dish like gumbo and thaw them while cooking. This is easiest to do if the

Nothing beats thawing in a refrigerator—for any frozen, raw food.

oysters were individually frozen in plastic ice cube trays. If they were frozen in water, the excess water may add too much liquid to the gumbo too late in the cooking process to boil it out.

Thawing oysters for cooking should be done in a refrigerator. Allow twelve hours for a one-pound package to thaw and eighteen hours for a two-pound package. Thawing under cold running water, an acceptable method for shell-on shrimp, is too harsh for soft-fleshed oysters. The action of the running water will leach away much flavor and likely damage the oysters' soft tissues.

No seafood product should ever be thawed at room temperature in the kitchen or in hot water. Thawing at room temperature allows degradation of the thawed edges while the center is still frozen. Hot water will denature an oyster's proteins and change its texture.

Oysters Beat the Rap on Cholesterol

For years, all shellfish, including crustaceans (crabs, shrimp, and crawfish) and mollusks (oysters, clams, and mussels) were branded as high in cholesterol. Doctors urged extreme moderation in shellfish consumption or even abstinence. All this has changed, especially for mollusks.

Crustaceans are still recognized as being relatively high in cholesterol compared to poultry, beef, pork, and lamb. More current research indicates, though, that crustacean cholesterol is harder for the human body to absorb than that of meat, eggs, milk, and cheese. Even if it wasn't, consumption of crustaceans can easily be fit into the American Heart Association's recommendation to limit daily cholesterol intake to 300 milligrams (mg) or less.

The big news is for oysters (and their cousins clams, mussels, octopus, and scallops). Oysters and other mollusks were being analyzed using outdated scientific methods that measured both real cholesterol (which is a sterol) and cholesterol-like substances called non-cholesterol sterols.

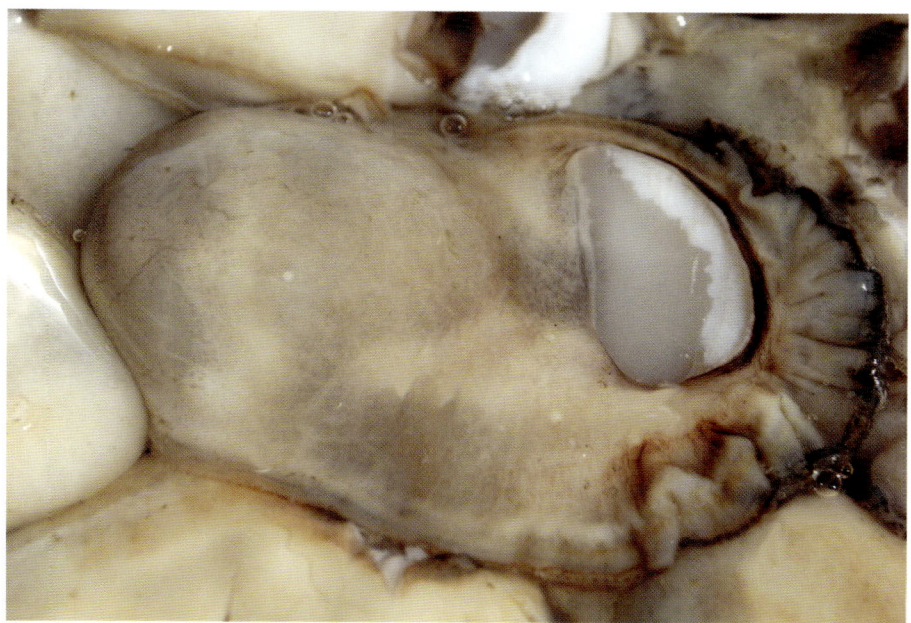

Because cholesterol makes up only 30 to 40 percent of the sterols found in mollusks (except for squid), modern cholesterol readings for these species are much lower than they used to be. Eastern oysters contain only 55 mg of cholesterol per 3½-ounce serving, compared to 80-95 mg of cholesterol for lean beef, pork, or lamb. Chicken, with or without skin, is only slightly less.

It is thought that these low cholesterol levels are due to oysters being vegetarians that feed by straining microscopic sea plants called phytoplankton from the water. Clams, mussels, octopus, and scallops are even lower in cholesterol than oysters. The low cholesterol levels in mollusks puts them on par with finfish, which are often recommended for diets because they are so low in cholesterol.

As mentioned earlier, the only mollusk still considered high in cholesterol is squid. At about 230 mg of cholesterol per 3½-ounce serving, squid are the only seafood, besides fish roe, to come close to eggs in cholesterol content.

Molluscan Shellfish Allergies

Seafood allergies, along with dairy and peanut allergies, are common in the United States. Four percent of Americans have some type of food allergy. Interestingly, seafood allergies are more common in populations that eat a lot of seafood than in those that eat little seafood. Also, raw seafood is a more powerful allergen than is cooked seafood, which is bad news for oyster-lovers.

People allergic to oysters have a molluscan shellfish allergy and almost always are also allergic to other mollusks, such as clams, mussels, snails, squid, and octopus. Other seafood allergies include allergies to crabs, shrimp, crawfish and lobsters (crustacean allergies), and finfish.

People allergic to mollusks may be allergic to crustaceans as well, and sometimes even finfish. Anyone showing an allergic reaction to any seafood should consult a doctor before attempting to eat any other seafood.

For very sensitive people, any exposure, including breathing cooking vapors or eating food fried in oil previously used to fry mollusks, can trigger what is known as an allergic cascade.

This happens when the immune system overreacts to a seafood

protein, believing it to be a dangerous substance. To combat the protein, the immune system releases antibodies into the bloodstream. These antibodies interact with blood mast cells and basophils to trigger the release of histamines and other chemicals into the blood.

It is the histamines and other chemicals that stimulate allergy symptoms. By causing blood vessels to swell and individual cells to leak fluid, histamines produce allergy symptoms such as itchiness, rash, hives, stomach cramps, nausea, and respiratory problems. Individuals who are sensitive to allergic seafood reactions even can go into life-threatening anaphylactic shock, which involves breathing problems and lowered blood pressure.

The only form of treatment for molluscan allergies is complete avoidance of the allergens—in this case, oysters, clams, mussels, snails, squid, and octopus.

Fish Oils and Oysters

Two Danish researchers, Hans Olaf Bang and Jorn Dyerberg, in the 1970s discovered that Greenland Eskimos ate a fattier diet than any other group in the world, but they had virtually no heart disease. The major reason, they discovered, was that besides eating a lot of whale and seal meat and blubber, the Eskimos ate a lot of fish.

Omega-3 fatty acids in oils in the fishes' bodies provided the heart protection. About seven different omega-3 (often abbreviated as n-3) fatty acids occur in fish oil. The two most important are eicosapentaenoic acid (EPA) and docosahexaenoic acid (DHA). Both are found mainly in fish oils. Further research has shown some of the specific effects of these n-3s on human ailments.

- Triglyceride levels can be reduced as much as 30 percent by consumption of n-3-rich fish oils. The American Heart Association recommends 2 to 4 grams of n-3s daily for people with high triglycerides.
- Studies have shown that men with the highest levels of n-3s in their

blood have an 80 percent lower risk of fatal, massive interruption of the heart's rhythm (sudden cardiac death) than men with the lowest blood levels.

- N-3s can lower both systolic and diastolic blood pressure.
- Treatment with n-3s has shown a reduction of the risk of death from atherosclerosis (hardening of the arteries) by 23 percent.

Generally speaking, fatty seafoods have more n-3s than lean seafoods and coldwater species have more n-3s than warmwater species. Within this generalization, however, eastern oysters do better than one might expect.

Oysters have more n-3s than bass, catfish, croaker, dolphin (mahi-mahi), black drum, flounder, groupers, speckled and white trout, sheepshead, red snapper, crabs, and crawfish. Although not as high in n-3s as dark-fleshed finfish such as mackerel and bluefish, oysters can still play an important component in the recommendation to eat two to fouras seafood meals per week.

How to Shuck an Oyster

(Press Knife Method)

Holding the oyster with one hand, insert an oyster knife firmly between the shell halves at the hinge end of the oyster. Avoid pointing the knife blade at the hand holding the oyster.

While maintaining firm but not excessive pressure on the knife, twist the handle in screw-driver-fashion until the hinge pops and separates.

At this point, the adductor muscle is still holding the two shell halves together and must be cut. To cut the muscle, insert the knife between the shells and scrape it firmly against the inside surface of the upper shell.

When the upper shell is released, gently remove and discard it.

To free the oyster from the bottom shell, cut the adductor muscle by scraping the knife across the point where the muscle is attached to the lower shell.

Never attempt to open an oyster by using the knife to lever directly up or down. The blade may break or the shell may shatter, causing injury to the person opening the oyster.

How to Shuck an Oyster

(Break Knife Method)

Use a hammer to break off enough of the bill of an oyster to expose a gap between the two shells. Don't break off more than is necessary, because this can damage the oyster meat and create excess shell particles.

Insert the oyster knife blade into the gap made with the hammer and cut the adductor muscle from the upper shell by scraping the muscle loose from the shell. Be careful not to rip through the center of the oyster and tear it.

When the upper shell is released, gently remove and discard it.

To free the oyster from the bottom shell, cut the adductor muscle by scraping the knife across the point where the muscle is attached to the lower shell.

Part II: Recipes

Huitres Marinade Buquet

I got this recipe in 1983, when Mike Voisin, owner of Motivatit Seafoods, an oyster-processing house in Houma, brought a couple gallons of them to a Concerned Shrimpers Association annual meeting. I think that I ate half of them myself. He credits the dish to his mentor, A. J. Bouquet, the near-legendary Houma oyster and shrimp canner. It is flavorful, but not spicy. The horseradish is a kiss on the cheek, not a slap in the face.

Tip: These make ideal shooters when served in shot glasses.

2 onions, chopped
1 cup ketchup
1 cup salad oil
1 tbsp. horseradish
1 tsp. onion puree
1 tsp. garlic puree
2 shallots, chopped
¼ cup chopped green olives
1 tbsp. vinegar
Tabasco sauce to taste
Salt and pepper to taste
2 lemons, squeezed (juice and carcasses)
1 gal. oysters with liquor

Blend all ingredients except oysters and liquor. Add oysters and enough liquor to make a thick marinade. Refrigerate 4 hours before serving. Serves 25-30 as hors d'oeuvres.

Marinated Oysters
a la For'-Rest

Tip: Forrest says don't buy oysters from a grocery store. Go to the shucking house to get unwashed oysters or shuck them yourself. Save and use the oyster liquor!

Tip: Forrest suggests that the serving bowl should be kept buried in ice, so that the oysters never get warm.

Forrest Travirca was a game warden—one of the first generation assigned to the Louisiana Department of Wildlife and Fisheries Oyster Strike Force. Oysters were his specialty and he soon attracted a following of other game wardens who relished this dish. For years Forrest would provide four to six gallons of these marinated oysters for his peers at the Louisiana Wildlife Agents Association meeting. These oysters are dressed up with all those goodies that Louisianans love.

1 gal. oysters with liqour
2 medium onions, chopped
2 7-oz. jars green olives, chopped
2 8-oz. cans tomato sauce
2 6-oz. cans black olives, chopped
1 large bell pepper, chopped
1½ cups chopped celery (use stalks from the heart of celery)
½ clove garlic, minced
2 tbsp. Worcestershire sauce
1 tbsp. soy sauce
Salt to taste
1 14-oz. can sliced mushrooms
2 16-oz. jars medium salsa
Tony Chachere's Original Creole Seasoning to taste

Mix all ingredients together with only enough oyster liquor to cover the oysters. The salsa will determine how spicy this dish is. If you like spicy food, use a hot salsa. If not, use medium or mild. For best results, let the oysters sit in the mix overnight in the refrigerator. Feeds an army.

Pickled Oysters

This recipe was sent to me to test for my LSU fisheries newsletter by an anonymous reader from South Carolina in 1979. Hide the jar in the back of your refrigerator for at least three days. The longer they are held, the sourer they become, but they are at their best before three weeks. It is normal for the pickling solution to become slightly milky after a few days. Pickled oysters were a very popular item during the Great Oyster Craze of the nineteenth century.

3 dozen fresh, medium-sized oysters
4 cups boiling water
1 medium red onion
2 red cayenne peppers
½ tbsp. whole peppercorns
1 bay leaf
½ cup cider vinegar
½ tsp. salt
1-2 dashes Tabasco sauce

Purge the oysters by dropping them in 4 cups of rapidly boiling water. Remove the saucepan from heat and let the oysters sit for about 5 minutes before draining them in a colander. Thinly slice the onion into rings and separate the rings. Cut the cayenne peppers in half lengthwise and scrape out the seeds and pulp. In a pint jar, begin layering the oysters, the onions, and the hot peppers along with peppercorns. Place a whole bay leaf about halfway up the jar. When the jar is full or as full as it is going to get, pour in the mixture of vinegar, salt, and Tabasco sauce. Serve as a pickle with meals or snacks.

Oysters Caminada Bay

This is the first of three appetizer recipes from the Barataria Restaurant, which once stood on Harrison Avenue in New Orleans. The restaurant was owned by Ralph "Buddy" Pausina and his son Ralph F. "Ralphie" Pausina. The Pausina family holds a prominent place in the oyster farming industry.

The recipe calls for using a salsa of your own choice. If you make your own salsa, Buddy recommends using Château de L'Hyvernière, a Muscadet-Sèvre et Maine wine, to provide the acid for the salsa. This dry white wine has long been recognized for its affinity for oysters and the celebration of the new vintage is held annually in New Orleans. The two Pausinas won a first place award, including a trip to France, from the winery for their cooking. Buddy describes the wine as "not pricy" and says it is available in the French section at Dorignac's Food Center near his home in Metairie.

24 large oysters on the half-shell
1⅓ cups salsa of your choice
2 tbsp. minced fresh cilantro
3 limes, cut into wedges

Open oysters and place on a plate on the half-shell. Spread a dollop of salsa on each half-shell oyster. Sprinkle with minced cilantro. Serve with lime wedges on the side to squirt on the oysters. Serves 4.

Oysters Ralphie

The second of the Barataria Restaurant trio of great appetizers is named after the junior Pausina, Ralphie. A trained chef, Ralph F. Pausina was part of the first class that Chef Paul Prudhomme put together. With the sale of their restaurant, Ralphie moved on to become executive chef for Pappas Bros., a Houston-based operation of about three hundred restaurants operating under several names. His erstwhile partner in Barataria Restaurant, father Ralph "Buddy" Pausina, is fully retired from both the oyster farming and restaurant businesses after oystering from 1960 to 2005. Buddy was a third generation oysterman, following his grandfather Vincent Pausina who immigrated from Donja Vrućica, when Croatia was under the rule of Austria. Cooking has been a long-time hobby for Buddy.

¼ tsp. dried oregano
1½ tsp. minced garlic
1½ tsp. lemon juice
4 oz. grated Romano cheese
1½ tbsp. beer
1¼ cups mayonnaise
¼ tsp. black pepper
1 tbsp. chopped parsley
12 oysters on the half shell

Make the Ralphie Sauce by combining all ingredients except oysters and mix well. Spoon approximately 1 tbsp. of sauce on each oyster, with less on small oysters. Bake at 350 degrees for 15 minutes. Serve while hot. Serves 4 as an appetizer.

Tip: The Ralphie Sauce is also very good when spread on bread like garlic butter and toasted in a toaster oven. The basic sauce recipe makes enough for 2 dozen oysters. It stores well.

Baked Oysters Bay Batiste

Tip: The Pausinas say to use whatever varieties of mushrooms are available.

Tip: Any leftover chorizo mix is excellent scrambled with eggs for breakfast or makes a rich sausage (not dressed) po-boy.

The only thing tricky about this dish is being sure that the right chorizo is used. Chorizos are simply pork sausages with a strong dose of pepper that hail from Spain, Portugal, or Latin America. In this part of the United States, most of what is available is either Spanish or Mexican. There are big differences between the two. In Spanish chorizo the meat is coarsely chopped, seasoned with smoked paprika, and then cured by smoking. It is ready to eat from the wrapper. In Mexican chorizo, the meat is ground, seasoned with mild chilies, and is *chorizo fresco,* meaning that it is uncured and uncooked. Mexican chorizo is usually removed from the casing, as it is in this recipe, before cooking. This dish calls for Mexican chorizo. Do not substitute Spanish chorizo. Glenda and I tend to buy local and we love high-quality food products. We recommend the chorizo marketed by Amato's Winery in Independence, Louisiana. It is low in fat and made from an authentic Mexican recipe.

½ lb. fresh Mexican chorizo
¼ small bell pepper
½ small onion
½ small carrot
3 cups assorted mushrooms (button, shitake, portobello), diced
1 tbsp. olive oil, (optional)
1 clove garlic, minced
1 tsp. chopped parsley
2 tbsp. breadcrumbs
12 oysters on the half shell
Parmesan cheese to taste

Bake chorizo at 350 degrees until just done. Take out of oven, remove casing from sausage, and save the grease. Puree the sausage in a food processor and set aside. Puree bell pepper, onion, and carrot in food processor and set aside. Sauté mushrooms until tender in the grease left over from sausage. If you don't have enough grease, add olive oil. Stir in garlic and parsley and sauté an additional minute. Remove from heat and add in the pureed sausage and vegetables. Add breadcrumbs and mix well. Top oysters with mix and sprinkle with Parmesan cheese. Bake in 350 degree oven for 15 minutes. Serves 4 as an appetizer.

The Secrets to Cooking Oysters

Some people maintain that the very best way to serve and eat oysters is raw on the half-shell, but oysters are indeed wonderful in cooked preparations. Cooked oysters are both bold and subtle in taste at the same time, and small things can make a big difference in the taste of a dish. The secrets to taking some of the mystique (and mistakes) out of cooking oysters are listed below.

- Don't overcook them. In soups and sauces, oysters should be added very near the end and cooked just long enough to release some, but not all, of their internal liquids into the dish. The longer they are cooked, the more they will shrink as they lose liquid. Overcooking occurs in a matter of minutes and the result is strong-tasting oysters with the rubbery mouth-feel of a lead pencil eraser. In liquids, the rule of thumb is to cook them only until the lips on the edges of the oyster curl. Perfectly fried oysters should still be creamy in their centers. Practice produces perfection in frying.
- Learn to shuck oysters yourself or buy unwashed oysters from shucking houses. Oyster liquor may be important for your dish. Liquor is the liquid that comes out of the shell as an oyster is shucked. It is not the liquid that commercially-packed oysters are packed with, although for cooking purposes this liquid is certainly better than plain water. Oysters processed in processing plants invariably are thoroughly washed and drained as part of the process to remove grit and shell and then repacked with tap water. The process produces beautiful oysters but no liquor. Liquor is not needed for fried or grilled preparations. However, for most others, its addition with the oysters is important and in some recipes it is necessary. Only by shucking oysters oneself, can every drop of this nectar be saved. Oyster liquor freezes very well.
- Be aware of salt. If all you ever cook with is washed oysters produced by commercial shucking houses, this precaution is unnecessary. But if you use unwashed oysters or shuck your own, the innate salt within the oysters can vary widely. Depending on where and when they were caught, oysters can range from blandly unsalted (sometimes called sweet) to intensely briny—the kind that raw-oyster lovers crave. But adding salt to salty oysters, as one would salt washed or sweet oysters, will result in a dish with too much salt, completely ruining it.

Learning to shuck your own oysters is easier than you think.

Angels on Horseback

This is an old recipe, but it's just as good now as it was in the nineteenth century. It is so good, I routinely eat the leftovers cold from the refrigerator. Besides its impressive taste, it is ever so easy to cook. I usually have people standing and waiting, plate in hand, for them to come off my barbeque grill. We prefer them grilled rather than baked in the over, although both are good

2 dozen large oysters
12 slices bacon
½ tsp. salt
⅛ tsp. pepper
⅛ tsp. paprika
2 tbsp. dried parsley

Drain the oysters and place each oyster across a half slice of bacon. In a small bowl mix the salt, pepper, paprika, and parsley. Stir to blend. Sprinkle the seasonings evenly over oysters. Wrap bacon around seasoned oyster and fasten with toothpick. Place the oysters on a rack over a shallow baking pan or on a broiling pan. Bake at 450 degrees until the bacon is just done. Alternatively, they may be grilled on an outdoor grill. Either way, do not overcook. The toothpicks may be removed before serving. Serves 4-6 as an appetizer.

Devils on Horseback

If you think angels on horseback are good, wait until you try this. I get wobbly just thinking about it. Jalapeño peppers are strange. If you eat a slice straight up, it burns like the dickens. Put that slice on a bite of food and cook it, and it is delightful. Angels on Horseback and this dish are two of the few dishes in which we prefer to use dried parsley over fresh. The English version of this dish calls for wrapping bacon around a wine-poached prune stuffed with an almond and mango chutney. Oh, how we love America!

2 dozen large oysters
12 slices bacon
12 slices canned jalapeño peppers
½ tsp. salt
¼ tsp. pepper
2 tbsp. dried parsley

Drain the oysters and cut the bacon slices in half. Place an oyster on each half slice, followed by a jalapeño pepper slice. Sprinkle the salt, pepper, and parsley evenly over each oyster. Roll the bacon around the seasoned oyster and pin with a toothpick. Place oysters on a broiling pan in a 450 degree oven or grill on a barbeque pit. Cook for 20 minutes, or until the bacon is almost crisp. The toothpicks may be removed before serving. Serves 4-6 as an appetizer.

Tip: Do not use fresh jalapeño peppers for this dish, because they will be too crunchy.

Oysters-a-Baken

Carolyn Falgout, who cooked this dish for us, and her husband Lenny own and operate a registered Brahman cattle breeding business near Amite, Louisiana.

"We eat beef and seafood," she says. Maybe it's because she produces both. She leases about 4,500 acres of waterbottom from the state to farm oysters, in addition to her cattle business. She said that the idea for this recipe came after eating rumaki. "I said that I bet that this would be good with oysters. I tried it on neighbors who came over for a crawfish boil. They kept asking, 'you got some more of those?' It's Cajun rumaki." The water chestnut adds an absolutely delightful crunch.

3 dozen large oysters
1½ cups Italian breadcrumbs
2 8-oz cans sliced water chestnuts
2 lb. sliced bacon

Roll oysters in breadcrumbs. Place a water chestnut slice on the top and bottom of each oyster. Wrap bacon slice around the oyster and water chestnuts and secure with a toothpick. Roll in breadcrumbs again and place in a baking dish. Bake at 375 degrees for 25-35 minutes. Check after 15 minutes and continue to check periodically. When the bacon is crisp and oysters are brown, remove from the oven. Serves 4 as an entrée or 8 as an appetizer.

Carolyn Falgout loves cattle as much as oysters.

Tip: Carolyn likes a strong bacon presence in this dish, but if you use small oysters, use only ½ slice of bacon per oyster.

Sautéed Oyster Crunches

Dudley Vandenborre of Slidell, Louisiana, calls himself "an oyster fanatic," claiming that they are the best by far of all seafoods. "It's no wonder the Romans hauled them everywhere they went 2,000 years ago." He gives credit to fishing pal Ed Sexton for the concept of this recipe. "Ed cooks fish this way at his camp in Port Eads. You don't have a real big mess to clean up and they are good." The exteriors have a light crunch and the interiors are creamy.

3 eggs
½ cup milk
5 dozen oysters
3 rolls Ritz crackers, crushed finely
¼ cup olive oil
Tony Chachere's Creole Seasoning to taste

Whip eggs and milk in a small bowl. Dip the oysters in the milk wash then roll them in the cracker crumbs. Heat olive oil in a non-stick pan. Add oysters and cook until brown. Turn and brown the other side. Remove from pan and sprinkle with Creole seasoning.

Imperial Oysters

Melanie Charpentier is from "down the bayou" in Lafourche Parish.

Tip: Melanie says to use whatever cheese you have on hand. Any cheese works well in this dish.

Tip: Oyster shell halves may be substituted for the cast-iron pans, but the excess butter should still be reserved for dipping.

Melanie Charpentier, the originator of this dish, was born and raised in Golden Meadow. She and her husband Robert have two homes: one "down the bayou" in Cut Off, Louisiana, which she calls "the main home," in spite of spending 95 percent of her time at her second home in River Ridge. Her youngest son, Jake, attends a high school in River Ridge from which middle son Luke, a 315-pound offensive lineman, graduated to get a football scholarship to the University of Arkansas. Melanie spent a year cooking Louisiana dishes for visiting college football coaches who were scouting her son. Rusty, her eldest son, is a supply boat captain for Odyssea Marine.

A serious cook, Melanie is a member of a Lafourche Parish cooking club that meets and cooks once a month. She credits her father for much of her cooking skills. "My mother never let me cook. She was afraid I would make a mess." She notes that her grandfather was a baker at that now defunct, but much beloved, Golden Meadow landmark, Dufrene's Bakery. "He and I used to cook a lot together, too. I especially remember blackberry dumplings."

2 dozen oysters
1 10-oz. package seasoned fish fry
Oil for frying
2 sticks butter
4 tbsp. minced garlic, prepackaged
1 cup mozzarella cheese
½ cup chopped green onions
French bread

Roll the oysters in fish fry to batter. Deep fry oysters in oil at 350 degrees until crispy and golden brown. Drain the oysters on paper towels to remove excess oil. In another pan, melt butter. Add garlic and stir to mix. Place fried oysters in garlic butter sauce and stir well to coat. Spoon 4 to 6 oysters into small cast-iron pans. Pour any leftover garlic butter sauce over oysters. Sprinkle mozzarella cheese and green onions over oysters and broil until the cheese melts and browns lightly. Serve in the individual pans. Sop up the garlic butter with French bread. Serves 4.

Drago's Charbroiled Oysters

Tip: It is important to get the fire as hot as possible for cooking the oysters. Flames are what this dish is all about.

Charbroiled oysters might be the most popular dish on the oyster scene in decades and Drago's Restaurant in Metairie started it all. Tommy Cvitanovich, who manages the family eatery, says that it is the simplest dish to cook at home, but also the most difficult to exactly duplicate. Tommy's parents, Drago and Klara, who were born in Croatia, opened their famous restaurant in 1969. Tommy invented the dish "about twenty years ago" with a sauce that he used for grilling redfish. He tried it on oysters and the rest is history. In the restaurant, the sauce is still used on black drum, shrimp, and mussels, either on the grill or in a skillet.

Drago's exact recipe has never been published, primarily, admitted Tommy, because he doesn't want to divulge the exact butter to margarine ratio in the recipe. But in a weak moment, he directed me to food critic Tom Fitzmorris's recipe, which, except for the butter-margarine thing, is the closest that anyone has come to the restaurant recipe. In fact, he says, that this is the one that he gives to friends who ask him for his recipe. Proud of the dish, he calls it "the best single bite of food in town."

2 lb. butter/margarine blend, melted
½ cup finely chopped fresh garlic
1 tbsp. black pepper
1 tsp. dried oregano
1 cup Parmesan cheese
1 cup Romano cheese
3 tbsp. chopped parsley
6 dozen oysters on the half shell

Heat a gas or charcoal grill as hot as you can get it. Mix butter blend with garlic, pepper, and oregano. In a separate bowl, mix the Parmesan cheese, Romano cheese, and parsley. Place the oysters on the half shell over the hottest part of the grill. Spoon the butter mixture liberally over the oysters. Add enough sauce so that much of it overflows into the fire and causes it to flare up. Liberally sprinkle cheese mixture over oysters. Repeat the butter and cheese steps again. The oysters are ready when they are browned, about 2-3 minutes.

The bottoms of the oyster shells will be almost black. Serve on shells immediately with hot French bread. Serves 8-12 as an appetizer.

Sup's Charbroiled Oysters

We call John Supan "Louisiana's Oyster Ambassador." He lives, eats, and breathes oysters. As an LSU research professor, all his professional time is spent working to produce the world's most perfect oyster. In his personal life, he cooks and eats oysters—lots of oysters. Everywhere he goes, he proselytizes for Louisiana oysters. In spite of maintaining that charbroiled oysters taste more like meat than like oysters, he admits that he and his wife Karen love them. In fact, he says that he doesn't know anyone who doesn't like them. Either a gas or charcoal grill may be used for this dish. John has modified his gas grill by removing its flame arrestors especially to cook this dish.

2 lb. butter
5 tbsp. minced garlic
1 tsp. black pepper
1 tsp. Italian seasoning
3 dozen oysters on the half shell
⅔ cup Parmesan cheese
⅔ cup Romano cheese
French bread

John Supan prepares charbroiled oysters often for his wife Karen.

Tip: Sup recommends using only butter, calling margarine "too watery."

Tip: The secret to this dish is to have the oysters engulfed in flames, so be sure the grill is very hot before placing the oysters on for cooking or the butter may not flare up.

Melt the butter in a saucepan. Add garlic, black pepper, and Italian seasoning and mix well. Place the oysters on the half shell on the grill. Mix the two cheeses and sprinkle the mixture liberally on the oysters. Spoon the butter over the oysters. Be sure to add enough butter at a time to run off the oysters and onto the hot coals to create flames. The flames cause smoke, which flavors the oysters. Repeat the butter spooning-process often. When the cheese on the oysters begins to brown, the oysters are done. Serve with French bread to sop up the sauce. Serves 4 as an appetizer.

Oyster Patties

This is one of Glenda's favorite recipes. But we can't take the credit for it, because she got it from Red Dudenhefer formerly of Lake Catherine, Louisiana, and currently of Picayune, Mississippi. Red's husband Milton was an oyster fisherman and shrimper. In later years they operated a shrimp-buying dock, also in Lake Catherine. This delicious recipe tastes baked, but isn't. It is ideal party food.

1 pt. oysters, with liquor
1 medium onion, finely chopped
1 tbsp. finely chopped celery
1 bunch green onions, finely chopped
1 tbsp. chopped bell pepper
2 tbsp. chopped parsley
1 clove garlic, minced
1 stick butter
5 tbsp. flour
1 bay leaf
1 tsp. salt
Dash red pepper
1 cup water
3 packages mini phyllo pastry shells

Drain the oysters and save the liquor. Sauté onions, celery, green onions, bell pepper, parsley, and garlic in butter until light brown. Add flour, stirring until well blended. Add oyster liquor, seasonings, and 1 cup water. Cook 5 to 10 minutes. Add oysters and cook until edges of oysters curl. Keep hot in a double boiler or on asbestos pad. If mixture gets too thick, add a little milk. It should be creamy but not runny. Spoon into pastry shells and serve. Serves 4-6.

Tip: Use small oysters or chop large oysters so they will fit in the pastry shells.

Oysters Edele

Don't try this dish if you don't have the juice, says chef Alex Patout.

Tip: When making the roux for this recipe, use ⅔ cup of flour and ⅓ cup oil instead of the usual ratio of 50:50.

Tip: Alex specifies the use of Tabasco sauce rather than other hot sauces because its flavor holds up well without making the dish too spicy.

Chef Alex Patout says that if you don't have "the juice," don't try to make this dish. The juice that he refers to is oyster liquor. The recipe calls for substantially more liquor than what will come from shucking the three dozen oysters used in the recipe. That means that you will have to raid your supply of frozen liquor, order extra liquor with your unwashed oysters, or rob some liquor from oysters used for another dish, like fried oysters, which don't use it. I first tried this prize-winning dish at a reception at the Boston Seafood Show in 1986 and loved it. I begged the recipe. But I learned the hard way that it won't work without enough juice. It tames the powerful roux flavor.

Alex was part of the wave of "Young Turks" who followed Chef Paul Prudhomme in revolutionizing New Orleans cooking. Prudhomme opened K-Paul's Louisiana Kitchen restaurant New Orleans in July of 1979. Alex opened Patout's Restaurant in New Iberia in November 1979, followed by Alex Patout's Restaurant in New Orleans in 1988. Prior to Prudhomme and Gang, the menus in the city's Creole restaurants all pretty much looked the same—dark gumbo, turtle soup, oysters rockefeller, shrimp rémoulade, trout amandine, and trout meuniere. Now, anything goes, as long as it tastes good.

Alex's New Orleans restaurant never reopened after Hurricane Katrina and he is now executive chef at Landry's Restaurant near his native New Iberia. He calls this dish a Patout family tradition, and indeed it is named after his father's only sister. The Patouts always made it on Christmas Eve. "The elegance of this dish," he says, "deserves a formal reception. Spoon enough into the pastry shells so that some sauce runs into the plate when they are cut. It's messy," says Alex, "but elegant—like Cajuns, messy, but elegant."

3 dozen unwashed oysters, with the liquor
12 Pepperidge Farm pastry shells
1 cup dark roux
3 cups oyster liquor
1 tsp. salt
1 tsp. red pepper
½ tsp. black pepper
½ tsp. white pepper
8-10 drops Tabasco sauce
1½ cups chopped green onion tops
½ cup chopped parsley

Drain oysters, reserve the liquor. Bake the pastry shells according to package directions. Remove the centers of the pastries and set them aside. Warm the roux in a black-iron skillet. Stir in 1½ cups oyster liquor. Gradually add more oyster liquor until you reach the consistency of a chocolate mousse. Once you reach this stage, add seasoning, onion tops, parsley, and oysters. Cook over medium-high heat, stirring continuously. Cook until the edges of the oysters are curled and the sauce thickens. Reduce until the last drop adheres to the edge of a tipped spoon. The mixture should be a little thicker than a stew. If too thick, add oyster juice. Adjust the seasonings before filling pastry shells. Serve immediately while hot. Serves 10-12.

A Taste for Cast Iron

Alex Patout loves cooking in cast-iron cookware. So do we. Anyone who cooks with cast iron or even just eats something cooked in cast ironware will tell you that foods cooked in it taste better. There are likely a number of reasons for this. Flavors of ingredients marry well in dishes cooked in *chaudière noire*—cast iron. Heat transfer is so good that few hot spots occur and scorching is reduced.

Cast iron browns meats exceptionally well before they are used in further preparations. With its superb heat transfer properties, it produces wonderful crusts in dishes like cornbread. But the most important reason for food tasting better when cooked in cast iron may be that cast iron gives up small quantities of its iron to the dish being cooked in it.

An article in the July 1986 *Journal of the American Dietetic Association* shows how much cast iron is added to various foods by cooking them in cast iron. The results, shown on the next page, are from cooking with seasoned pieces. They found that foods cooked in new iron pieces absorbed even more.

Besides being the original non-stick cookware, cast iron makes food taste better, too.

Foods tested (100 g./3 oz.)	Iron content when raw (in mg.)	Iron content after cooking in iron skillet (in mg.)
Applesauce, unsweetened	0.35	7.38
Spaghetti sauce	0.61	5.77
Chili with meat and beans	0.96	6.27
Medium white sauce	0.22	3.30
Scrambled egg	1.49	4.76
Spaghetti sauce with meat	0.71	3.58
Beef vegetable stew	0.66	3.40
Fried egg	1.92	3.48
Spanish rice	0.87	2.25
Rice, white	0.67	1.97
Pan-broiled bacon	0.77	1.92
Poached egg	1.87	2.32
Fried chicken	0.88	1.89
Pancakes	0.63	1.31
Pan-fried green beans	0.64	1.18
Pan-broiled hamburger	1.49	2.29
Fried potatoes	0.42	0.80
Fried corn tortillas	0.86	1.23
Pan-fried beef liver with onions	3.10	3.87
Baked cornbread	0.67	0.86

Iron is an essential nutrient in human diets. It is used to form hemoglobin, which carries oxygen in red blood cells. Iron deficiencies cause anemia, the most obvious symptom of which is excessive tiredness. Iron deficiencies have been associated with a disorder known as pica. People with pica have a craving to eat non-food items, very often paper, but also ice, chalk, dirt, clay, and laundry starch, among other things.

Iron deficiencies occur among adults most often in women and athletes. Cooking in cast iron, as a method of adding iron to diets, is recommended by sports doctors and trainers.

Big Lake Oysters Rockefeller

Big Lake is the local name for Calcasieu Lake, a saltwater lake in southwestern Louisiana. Mary Poe, who cooked this dish for us, owns Big Lake Guide Service with her husband Jeff. The pair, along with their son Nick, actively guide fishermen and waterfowl hunters year round from their base at Hebert's Summer Place.

Mary says that this dish is more of a special preparation for them rather than an everyday meal. "But we just love it," she adds. I asked Jeff, who is a native of central Alabama, if he ate it growing up. "No" he drawled, "they sure didn't have it in the hills of Alabama. Nooo, my momma never ate it." Mary teases her husband. "Milk gravy, corn bread, fried okra, and fried corn." That's what they eat. "It's all good though, except for my cornbread. A dog wouldn't eat it."

Mary explains that canned spinach is just fine for the dish because it will be pureed anyway. She likes to "go light" on the breadcrumbs and Parmesan cheese. "I want to taste the green stuff." Jeff, in the background echoes, "Green is good!"

Mary Poe is equally skilled with a cooking spoon or a fishing rod.

Tip: The anchovy is an important ingredient in this dish. Don't omit it. But, adding more than one will make the dish fishy.

Tip: Squeeze the spinach until dry so that it won't make the sauce too thin when added to other ingredients.

2 dozen oysters, liquor reserved
1 4-lb. box rock salt
2 13½-oz. cans spinach, drained
1 canned anchovy
¾ tbsp. Worcestershire sauce
1 stick butter, melted
1 tbsp. lemon juice
¼ cup chopped celery
¼ cup chopped green onions
¼ cup chopped onions
¼ cup chopped parsley
1 tsp. anise seeds
1 tsp. salt
½ tsp. black pepper
5 drops Tabasco sauce
⅔ cup Italian breadcrumbs
⅔ cup freshly grated Parmesan cheese

Place oysters in half shells on a bed of rock salt and bake at 350 degrees until the edges of the oysters curl. Leave the juice in the oyster shells after baking. Puree the drained spinach in a food processor. Add all other ingredients, except breadcrumbs and Parmesan cheese, and continue to puree. If the mixture is too thick, add a little oyster liquor. Spoon the spinach mixture over the oysters, covering them with sauce. Sprinkle with Italian breadcrumbs and Parmesan cheese. Bake at 350 degrees for 20 minutes.

Smoked Oysters

When you try this little gem, you will never again want to eat canned, smoked oysters imported from China or Korea. Those taste like smoky pencil erasers. These are moist and succulent with a great mouth-feel. This is a dish to cook on a true side-smoker or a Green Egg, not a barbecue pit or grill. Low temperatures and lots and lots of smoke are the keys to success. The process is a little lengthy, so you need to allow four hours for preparation before the one-hour smoking process begins. Sometimes I will do the brining and rinsing the day before I smoke them. They store well overnight in the refrigerator.

Smoking Marinade

36 large oysters
2¼ cups water
¾ cup kosher salt
¾ cup brown sugar
1 cup chopped green onion, tops and bottoms
1 tbsp. ground oregano

Check oysters for shell particles and set aside. Mix all the remaining ingredients and stir well to dissolve the salt and sugar. Add the oysters and set aside at room temperature for 30 minutes. Be sure that all the oysters are submerged in the marinade. Line a platter with several layers of paper towels, rinse the oysters, pat them dry, and spread them on paper towels. Allow them to air dry for 1 hour. Change the towels if they become soaked by liquid from the oysters.

Smoked Oysters

¾ cup kosher salt
⅓ cup brown sugar
1 tbsp. onion powder
1½ tsp. ground oregano
Olive oil

Tip: Because smoking results in a great deal of shrinkage, the largest oysters obtainable are the best ones to use for smoking.

Tip: Be sure to rinse the oysters thoroughly when a rinse is called for, or they will be too salty.

Combine the ingredients in a bowl. Remove the oysters from the platter and re-line it with new paper towels. Dip both sides of the oysters in the mix and place them on the towels. Allow them to air dry at room temperature for 1 hour. Rinse the oysters again, pat them dry and return them to a platter lined with new paper towels to air dry for 1 more hour. At this stage, the oysters should have a glossy appearance. Spread the oysters on a perforated grill plate or pan and place in a smoker at a temperature of 200 to 225 degrees. Place the oysters as far from the fire as possible. Cook for about 1 hour or until they have shrunken somewhat and appear dried, but not shriveled or hard. Remove the oysters from the smoker and put in a small bowl. Cover them with olive oil and store in the refrigerator. Serve at room temperature with crackers. Serves 6 as an appetizer.

Easy Oyster Dip

Tip: This dish can be made ahead of time and stored, because it freezes well.

This dish really rocks. It makes a generous amount and is at home at any Saints football party—or for that matter, any party. We have used it for more than fifteen years.

1 10-oz. pkg. frozen, chopped broccoli
1 large onion, chopped
½ cup butter
1 4-oz. can mushrooms, drained and chopped
1 10¾-oz. can cream of mushroom soup
1 6-oz. roll garlic cheese
½ 3-oz. roll jalapeño cheese
1 cup chopped oysters

Prepare broccoli according to package directions. Sauté onion in butter until tender. Add all other ingredients and cook over low heat until the cheese is melted. Serve with crackers. Serves 6-8.

Mama's Oyster Milk Soup

This recipe was originally Claire Fagan's. She handed it down to her daughter Patsy, who married Buddy Pausina, a prominent New Orleans-based oyster farmer for forty-five years. Buddy's father Baldo, usually called Capt. Baldo, is respected as one of the oystermen who helped the industry develop to its present status. Buddy knows and appreciates good food. He spent a lot of time cooking on his oyster boat and as he says, "Why cook junk when you can eat good food?" This delicate dish has a silky mouth-feel.

4 green onions, chopped
2 cloves garlic, minced
1 stick butter
1 pt. oysters
½ tsp. celery salt
1 14-oz. can chicken stock
2 pt. heavy whipping cream
½ tsp. nutmeg

Sauté onions and garlic in butter until tender. Add oysters and cook until the edges curl. Add celery salt, chicken stock, and nutmeg. Heat and stir until near boiling. Add whipping cream, and heat until warmed through. Serve with a slice of toasted, buttered French bread floating in the soup. Serves 4.

Capt. John's Oyster Soup

I got this recipe in 1980 from the late John Alario of Westwego. John was one of five brothers and four sisters, all of whom were involved with the seafood industry in one way or another. John worked on the shrimp trawler *Barnacle Bill* for many years before skippering the Alario family's freight boats, the *Alario Bros.* and the *CWC*. In those days, trawl boats were small and didn't carry ice to ice their shrimp catches. John would make one drag in the morning, then begin to take on and ice the small trawler's catches. After using all the ice available on the boat, the freight boat would begin the long slog from lower Barataria Bay to the shrimp canneries in Westwego. This savory recipe is creamy and smooth even though it contains no dairy products. Don't let the amount of celery in the recipe scare you out of trying it. The dish is simple, easy to prepare, and sure to impress your guests.

2 medium onions, chopped
4 tbsp. butter
2 pt. oysters
2 10¾-oz. cans cream of celery soup
2 soup cans of water
2 tsp. chopped parsley
Salt and pepper to taste
Paprika (optional)

Sauté the onions in butter until tender. Add oysters and cook for about 15 minutes until the oysters are browned. Add cream of celery soup, both cans of water, and parsley. Cook until oysters are tender, about 15 minutes. Salt and pepper to taste. Garnish with paprika. Serve with crackers or French bread. Serves 6.

Lucy's Louisiana Oyster Soup

Like with so many good recipes, I had to play detective to get this one. Westwego, Louisiana, shrimper Jimmy Frickey reported to me in 1999 that he had just eaten the best oyster soup he had ever tried in his life. The soup was prepared by Andrea (Andy) Galiano, but I couldn't locate her. I found out that her mother lived in Amite, Louisiana, and was able to get Andy's telephone number from her. Andy bounced credit for the recipe back to her grandmother, Lucy Kass. Years later she told me that Jimmy still calls her once a year and asks her to prepare it for him. This recipe is unusual for oyster soups, because it is a red, tomato-based preparation.

½ cup cooking oil
5 medium onions, chopped
1 6-oz. can tomato paste
1 tbsp. sugar
6 cloves garlic, minced
1 stalk celery, coarsely chopped
2 qt. water
3 oz. thin spaghetti
1 qt. oysters
Salt and pepper

Add cooking oil to a large pot and heat. Add onions and sauté until medium brown. Add tomato paste and sugar, and simmer over low heat at least 30 minutes. Add garlic, celery, and water. Boil until celery is tender. Add spaghetti and oysters. Cook until spaghetti is tender. Salt and pepper to taste. Serves 6.

Baba Neda's Oyster Soup

Tip: If the soup needs a flavor boost, add a chicken bouillon cube.

This dish harkens back to simpler, but at the same time more challenging, days when Croatian oyster fishermen and their families lived deep in the marsh near their all-important oyster leases, which they cultivated and watched day and night. None of these homes, which we would call camps today, had electricity or refrigeration, so everything was cooked with what could be caught fresh, raised nearby, or easily stored without spoiling. The recipe is Neda Jurisich's and was prepared for us by her daughter Eva Vujnovich. It is comfort food at its best definition.

1 qt. oysters, with liquor
1 12-oz. package very thin pasta
¼ cup olive oil
2 medium onions, finely chopped
5 cloves garlic, minced
1 bunch green onions, finely chopped
5 medium potatoes, cut in ½-inch cubes
Salt and pepper to taste
1 chicken bouillon cube, (optional)

Drain oysters and set aside. Save the liquor. Cook pasta according to package directions. Pour olive oil into a large pot. Add onions, garlic, and green onions. Sauté until tender and light brown. Add potatoes and sauté until tender, stirring frequently. Add oyster liquor, salt and pepper, and cooked pasta. Simmer 10-15 minutes. Add bouillon cube if desired. If more liquid is needed, add water. Stir in oysters and cook an additional 30-40 minutes. Serves 6.

Baba Neda's Story

The stories of south Louisiana's Croatian immigrants and the state's oyster industry are so closely intertwined as to be almost inseparable. Neda Jurisich's story is illustrative. Known as Baba Neda (baba means grandmother in Croatian) to her nine American grandchildren, Neda Taliancich was born in 1904, in the town of Igrane, which was controlled by the Austro-Hungarian Empire at the time. Later in her life, before she emigrated to America, her home country became Yugoslavia.

Life for the girl's family was hard during and following World War I and two of her brothers, Peter and Leopold, had already left the country for a new life along the lower Mississippi River in Louisiana. One day a young Croatian man in Louisiana, Frank Jurisich, paid a visit to the two brothers and spied a framed photograph of Neda on a fireplace mantle. He liked what he saw and asked about her. Jurisich told them that he would like to marry her.

The brothers wrote her with the news and described America as a prosperous land, free of the privations of her homeland. Frank went to Yugoslavia to meet her and apparently wasn't disappointed. After a one-month courtship, the two were married and sailed for the United States. The year was 1928.

When they arrived in New Orleans, Neda stayed with her brother in New Orleans for a few weeks and Frank returned to his oyster camp on Bayou La Chute, in the marshes near Empire. No roads led to Empire then, and when the young bride traveled south to meet her husband, she did so by train. Frank met her in his small boat to take her to their home.

Her first sight of the humble camp that was to be her home shocked her, but she had made her choice. Besides, she had few options. In 1929 she gave birth to their daughter Eva and less than two years later to son Mitch. Both children were delivered by a midwife at her brother's home. Both times she made the trip back to Bayou La Chute.

Baba Neda, shown here on a typical tonging boat of the time, tonged oysters as well as most men. (Courtesy of Eva Vujnovich)

Seed oysters had to be bedded by hand, with shovels. Frank worked one side of the boat and Neda the other, and Frank was hard pressed to keep up with his wife. (Courtesy of Eva Vujnovich)

"She had such a hard time. There was no money in those days. Oysters were fifty cents a sack and you had to shine them like gold to sell them," Eva says. She managed the family with little money. She planted vegetables and fruit trees on dirt hauled in by Frank to spread on top of the oyster shells their home was built on and she fished the waters around the camp for seafood for the family to eat.

By 1936, the Jurisichs had saved enough money to buy a plot of land in Empire and build a house to allow the children access to a school. But Neda didn't sit back. Soon she began to work with her husband on their oyster boat. Oystering in those days was hard work; nothing was mechanized.

"She worked better than a man," says Eva proudly. "Culling oysters—she was fast. Shoveling oysters—she was fast. She would take one side of the boat and Dad the other. He had a hard time to keep up."

Neda continued to work on the family boat until the 1960s. Frank's death in 1965 took her off the boat permanently. She died at age ninety-seven in January 2002.

Oyster and Artichoke Soup

Soups made with oysters and artichokes have grown to become a Creole cooking tradition. This recipe is excellent, but I think I got carried away with quantities. It makes a big pot of soup. Be sure to allow enough preparation time to chop all of the ingredients. Finally, using oyster liquor is a must! If you shuck your own oysters, you can get the required amount from a sack. If you are buying your oysters, it is going to be more difficult to get the quart required for this recipe, but I promise that it is worth the effort.

2 sticks butter
1½ cups finely chopped onions
1 cup finely chopped celery
1 bell pepper, finely chopped
6 cloves garlic, minced
1 13.75-oz. can artichoke bottoms, chopped
1 cup flour
1½ qt. chicken stock
1 qt. oyster liquor
1 14-oz. can artichoke hearts, chopped
1 qt. oysters
1 cup chopped parsley
1 cup chopped green onion
1 pt. heavy cream
Salt and white pepper to taste

In a large pot, melt butter over medium heat. Add onions, celery, bell pepper, garlic, and artichoke bottoms and sauté until they are soft and clear. Add flour gradually, stirring constantly until blended. Add chicken stock and then oyster liquor gradually, while stirring constantly to blend. Add artichoke hearts. Bring soup to a simmer and cook for 30 minutes. Add oysters, parsley, green onions, and heavy cream. Cook until oysters firm up and the edges begin to curl. Season to taste with salt and pepper. Serves 6.

Creole Bouillabaisse

A bouillabaisse is a seafood soup that Mediterranean fishermen's wives made from the unsold or least salable odds and ends of their husbands' catches. Beyond that, we don't claim that this is an authentic bouillabaisse. Our seasoning package doesn't include orange peel, fennel, and saffron as the French recipes do and some people maintain that their absence alone is enough to deny the name bouillabaisse to the dish. Supposedly, three and preferably four different kinds of fish should be used—a lean fish, a firm fish, a soft-fleshed fish, and a gelatinous fish—but in this shellfish-crazed state we have pared the list to one. Almost any assortment of fish and shellfish can be used, so feel free to substitute. They only thing that we guarantee is that the basic recipe is very good with whatever seafood you use.

¼ cup flour
¼ cup cooking oil
1 cup chopped onion
½ cup chopped celery
2 cloves garlic, minced
¼ cup chopped parsley
1 qt. chicken broth
2 14.5-oz. cans diced tomatoes
1 cup dry white wine
1 tbsp. lemon juice
1 bay leaf
1 tsp. salt
½ tsp. red pepper
1 lb. fish fillets, cut up
1 pt. shucked oysters
1 lb. peeled shrimp

In a large pot over medium heat, make a roux by slowly blending flour and oil, stirring constantly until mixture is light brown. Add onions, celery, garlic, and parsley and continue stirring until vegetables are tender. Gradually stir in chicken broth. Add tomatoes, wine, lemon juice, and seasonings. Bring to a boil, then simmer for 10 minutes. Add fish and oysters and simmer for 5 minutes. Add shrimp and cook for 5 minutes more or until all seafood is done. Serve with freshly baked bread and seasoned olive oil for dipping. Serves 8.

P&J's Oyster Rockefeller Soup

I got my first recipe for this dish from Al Sunseri of the P&J Oyster Company in New Orleans in 1988, right after it won first place in the soup division of the *New Orleans Times-Picayune's* annual cooking contest. Then in 2010, **The P&J Oyster Cookbook** was published and the recipe was different—and they called it a bisque. Glenda and our cooking buddy Ginger Corkern began working on the two recipes in our kitchen, trying out different variations. This is what they came up with. Delicious!

1 qt. oysters, with liquor
2 stalks celery
¼ head iceberg lettuce
2 10-oz. boxes frozen spinach leaves, defrosted
3 green onions
2 cloves garlic
4 tbsp. butter
¼ tsp. cayenne pepper
½ cup Herbsaint, Pernod, or Anisette liquor
¾ cup fresh grated Romano cheese
Juice of 2 lemons
2 pt. half-and-half
Salt to taste
1 tbsp. Creole seasoning

Drain oysters, strain the liquor, and set aside. Chop celery, lettuce, spinach, green onions, and garlic in a food processor. Sauté chopped ingredients in butter in a large skillet for about 10 minutes over medium-low heat, stirring occasionally. Meanwhile, poach oysters in liquor until their edges curl, about 4 minutes. Add cooked oyster liquor and cayenne pepper to sautéed ingredients and stir. Chop 2 dozen poached oysters in a food processor, and add to sautéed ingredients. Stir in the liquor of your choice, Romano cheese, lemon juice, and half-and-half. Heat on medium-low heat for about 15 minutes, stirring occasionally. Season to taste with salt, pepper, and Creole seasoning. Add whole poached oysters before serving. Serves 8 generously.

Chicken Mix Gumbo

Tip: Always serve this with pepper vinegar, which can be added to taste at the table. Andy considers it a necessity with this dish.

Tip: The most important thing about this recipe is to brown the onions on medium-high heat. Tend closely at the end. The onions should be dark brown, but not burned.

"We love food in our family," says Andrea "Andy" Galiano. "In fact, my mother named me after Chef Andrea Apuzzo, owner of Andrea's Restaurant in Metairie. I learned to cook from my grandmother. When my mother moved out of town, Maw Maw would stay with us a couple of weeks at a time. When I would come home from work, she would show me how to cook. If it wasn't for Maw Maw Lucy, I would never have learned to cook.

"I was born and raised in Westwego. That was all I knew until I moved to Tangipahoa Parish. I thought that people were crazy for living up here, but [Hurricane] Katrina changed all that. My first job was at my grandfather's oyster factory. I would stamp the expiration dates on the caps. I got oyster water for customers and gave the shuckers the chips that they used to keep track of how many oysters they shucked."

This is a most unusual gumbo. It has no roux, but it looks and tastes like gumbo. All the color and taste come from browning the onions. Gumbos were cheap soups back in the day. Every family had a flock of chickens, hence the hen used in the recipe. The luncheon meat in this gumbo was probably an extender, similar to the boiled eggs that many rural Cajuns added to gumbos.

4 large onions, chopped
1 cup cooking oil
3-4 lb. hen, deboned and cut into bite-size pieces
Water
2 lb. sausage
½ cup chopped green onions
¼ cup chopped parsley
3 bay leaves
3 lb. luncheon meat
½ gal. oysters, with liquor
¼ cup Worcestershire sauce
Salt, red pepper, black pepper, and filé powder to taste

In a large pot, brown onions in cooking oil until dark brown. Add chicken and 1 cup water, and simmer until onions disappear. Add sausage, green onions, parsley, and bay leaves. Add water to half-fill the pot and let boil for 45 minutes or until the chicken is tender. Add luncheon meat and boil another 30 minutes. Stir in oysters with their liquor, Worcestershire sauce, and seasonings to taste. Serves 15.

Victor's Can't Miss Seafood Gumbo

Gumbos are a staple in south Louisiana diets. Anyone who has eaten gumbos knows that there is a big difference between one gumbo and another. This is an excellent, basic, seafood gumbo recipe. A traditional Cajun dish, it is not as dark as many New Orleans gumbos. If you prefer using gumbo crabs (crabs in the shell) rather than picked crabmeat, seven to ten average-sized crabs are the equivalent of a pound of meat. This recipe was contributed by Victor Adam of Gretna, Louisiana. Victor is an avid fisherman and cook.

⅓ cup flour
⅓ cup oil
3 onions, chopped
1 bell pepper, chopped
4 stalks celery, chopped
3 cloves garlic, minced
2 qt. water
2 bay leaves
Salt and pepper to taste
2 lb. peeled shrimp
1 lb. crabmeat
1 pt. oysters
Cooked rice
Filé powder

Make a roux by cooking the flour in the oil over medium heat until dark brown. Stir constantly to prevent burning. When the flour is browned, add onions, bell pepper, celery, and garlic and simmer, stirring constantly. When the vegetables are glossy, add water, bay leaves, and salt and pepper to taste. Cook on low heat for 30 minutes. Add shrimp and cook 15 minutes. Add crabmeat and oysters and cook another 15 minutes. Turn off heat and set aside at least 1 hour before serving. Reheat if necessary. Serve over rice. Add filé to individual bowls if desired. Serves 4-6.

Dudley's Deadly Fried Ones

This recipe comes to us from Dudley Vandenborre, the well-known Lake Pontchartrain fishing guide and lure-maker, who is best known by the moniker "Deadly Dudley." He is especially proud of his fried oysters. "These stay crispy all the time. Others, when you bring them in—they get soggy." Dudley attributes the crispiness of his oysters to the flour on the inside of the coating providing a barrier to moisture getting to the fish fry on the outside.

Cooking oil for frying
⅔ cup flour
1 cup buttermilk
1½ pt. oysters, drained
1 10-oz. bag Louisiana New Orleans Style Seasoned Fish Fry

Heat the oil to between 350 and 375 degrees. Mix flour and buttermilk to make a batter the consistency of pancake mix. Dip the oysters in the flour/buttermilk batter and coat evenly. Roll the battered oysters in the fish fry. Put the oysters in the fry basket and shake off any excess fish fry. Fry until golden brown, about 1½ minutes. Remove oysters from basket and drain on paper towels. Serves 4.

Dudley Vandenborre presents his theories behind frying oysters.

Italian Fried and Baked Oysters

The size of Carolyn Falgout's walk-in pantry tells you how much she loves to cook.

Tip: Watch the oysters carefully during frying because pancake batter doesn't brown as much as fish fry. When the edges of the oyster curl, they are done.

This is another recipe from Carolyn Kass Falgout, the beef and oyster lady and a delightfully original cook. She says that the first time she tried this, it was with left-over fried chicken. "I was puzzled about what to do with cold chicken besides eat it cold. The family loved it. I am a fanatic for anything garlic, so that's where the garlic came in." She stresses the use of pancake batter in this dish, saying that it is softer and has a sweeter taste than breading mix. "It is not as coarse and hard on the palate. Also, the pancake batter keeps it moist."

Carolyn shows her genetically superior Brahman cattle all over the world and has been to Thailand, Brazil, Mexico, Ecuador, Columbia, and Australia. Carolyn cooks at cow shows. "I started frying seafood next to my cows in the stalls in the cow barns for us to eat. Other showmen began asking me to cook. They know me for my oysters. Everywhere I go, they tell me to bring oysters.

"I started buying electric frying pans, crock pots, and lots of electrical cords. Now I bring five ice chests of seafood, beef, already cut-up seasonings, and two helpers. I talk to customers and I cook. Cooking is a big deal at the Houston Livestock Show. We have a buffet," she chuckles. "There is no difference between oyster farming and cattle farming. We are all the same people. When cattle people come to our home, we put on a seafood feast."

Carolyn grew up and milked cows on her grandfather's dairy farm in what is now Marrero, Louisiana. In spite of her love for cattle, Carolyn has never left her roots in the seafood industry. She and her brother Buster Kass, and before them her father, William Kass III, owned and operated an oyster-shucking house in nearby Westwego. The family also owned oyster boats and oyster farming leases, which are currently managed in partnership with another oysterman.

4 eggs
Salt and pepper to taste
4 dozen oysters, drained
4 cups Aunt Jemima Complete Buttermilk Pancake and Waffle Mix
Oil for frying
2 tbsp. chopped parsley
10 cloves garlic, minced
2 sticks unsalted butter
1 cup mozzarella cheese

In a small bowl, make an egg wash by beating eggs with salt and pepper. Dip oysters in egg mixture, dredge them in pancake mix, and then fry in oil at 350 degrees. When oysters are brown, remove from frying pan, drain on paper towels, and then place in an ovenproof pan. In another pan, sauté parsley and garlic in butter until the garlic is brown and tender. Drizzle the butter mixture over the oysters. Sprinkle with mozzarella cheese and bake at 375 degrees until the cheese has melted. Serves 4.

Perfect Deep Fried Oysters

There are a lot of ways to serve oysters, but to many purists the very best ways are the simplest: raw or deep fried. A perfectly fried oyster is hard to beat—crunchy on the outside; creamy on the inside. It sounds like such a simple dish and it is. But if it is, why are there so many bad fried oysters? Our biggest secret to frying oysters can be said in two words: Pitman Fryer. These wonderful propane-powered outdoor fryers, built in Dixie Inn, near Ruston, Louisiana, can help a novice cook look like a pro—if he or she watches the thermometer closely and never lets the temperature of the oil get below 350 degrees or above 375 degrees.

It is important to anticipate what the fryer will do and adjust the heat before the temperature drops or rises beyond the critical points. The large volume of oil in these fryers is part of their secret. Dropping a lot of seafood into them hardly lowers the oil temperature at all, something that tabletop fryers struggle with. Cooking oil stores remarkably well in these fryers between uses.

2 pt. oysters
1 10-oz. box seasoned fish fry
Salt and pepper, (optional)
Cooking oil for deep frying

Drain oysters and check for shell fragments. Pour fish fry into a medium bowl. If the oysters have been washed, salt and pepper may be mixed with the fish fry. Taste a small pinch to judge if the seasoning is right. Roll oysters, a few at a time, in the fish fry until evenly coated. Repeat until all oysters are coated. Drop them separately into the fish fryer basket that is immersed in hot oil. Putting the oysters in the basket and then lowering the basket into the oil can result in the oysters sticking to each other or to the basket. Deep-fryer baskets are best used to remove fried seafood from the oil, not add it. Do not add oysters until the oil is a minimum of 350 degrees and reduce the heat if the temperature is creeping upward to exceed 375 degrees. Fry in oil until golden, but not dark brown. Do not overcook! Remove the basket from the oil to its hanger and allow it to drain. Remove oysters to paper towels for further draining. Serve warm. Serves 6-8.

Pitman fryers come in single and double basket versions.

Tip: Use the brand of fish fry that suits your tastes. Fish fries differ from each other not only by the kinds and amounts of seasonings in the seasoned versions, but in the coarseness of the grind. Some are grainy; others are ground fine.

Glenda's Pink Tartar Sauce

Complimenting this recipe perfectly is Glenda's Pink Tartar Sauce. She is the Tartar-Sauce Queen and loves it with all fried seafood. For a long time, she couldn't find what she wanted in commercially prepared products, so she began experimenting thirty years ago. This is what she developed. It is unique and we have been using it ever since. This recipe makes a quart, but it stores well in the refrigerator.

⅓ cup chopped green onions
½ cup chopped celery
1 pt. mayonnaise
½ cup sweet relish
½ tsp. dry mustard
½ cup ketchup

Chop onions and celery finely in a food processor. Add mayonnaise, relish, dry mustard, and ketchup and whip until well blended.

Mama Vilka's Special Oysters

George Barisich demonstrates his tip for the day.

Tip: To prevent the formation of what he calls "dough-balls," George coats his oysters with fish fry by shaking them up in a gallon-size plastic zipper-type bag. He uses unseasoned fish fry for this dish.

George Barisich calls these "Special Oysters" because his mother only made them with olive oil when company came over. "She would plain-fry for us. We would ask her, 'Mama, aren't we good enough for special oysters?' We would eat whatever we were catching at the time—shrimp, oysters, or fish—whatever was in season. We had a lot of fried food. It was quick."

The olive oil that George used to glaze the oysters when he cooked them for us was from the Barisich family property near Sucuraj on the Croatian Island of Hvar in the Adriatic Sea. But he said that any olive oil will do. He was more particular about the brands of fish fry and cooking oil that he used. "I tried all the cheap stuff after Katrina. They weren't the same as Crisco."

Although George holds a college degree and has 1½ years of law school under his belt, his heart has always been in commercial fishing for shrimp and oysters. He is president of the United Commercial Fishermen's Association; past-president, past-chairman of the board, and current board member of the Louisiana Shrimp Association; and one of the founders of the Commercial Fishermen of America.

⅔ **cup olive oil**
¼ **cup chopped curly-leafed parsley**
5 **cloves garlic, minced**
2 **pt. oysters**
1 **10-oz. box Zatarain's Fish Fri**
½ **tsp. garlic salt**
½ **tsp. black pepper**
Crisco oil for frying

Mix the olive oil, parsley, and garlic in a small bowl and set aside. Drain and rinse oysters and set aside. Mix fish fry, garlic salt, and black pepper in a gallon zipper bag. Add oysters, a few at a time, and shake to coat evenly. Heat oil until hot over medium-high heat in a deep pan. Remove enough oysters from the bag to cover the bottom of the pan, and add them to the hot oil. Fry until they are golden brown and the edges of the oysters are curled. Remove oysters and drain on paper towels for 2 minutes, then put them in a large bowl.

Whisk the olive oil mixture and spoon some of it over the oysters. Toss the oysters gently by hand while still hot to coat them with the oil mixture. Repeat until all oysters are fried. Serve quickly before the oil makes the oysters soggy. Serves 4.

Saddleback Oysters

Charlie Lieux's (pronounced LEER, believe it or not) friends named this dish for him. It is a staple at his LSU parties, but he says he really doesn't need much excuse to cook it. Charlie, a master speckled trout fisherman, says his number one way to eat oysters is raw. "I eat ten sacks a year; I want them only with their own juice; I want them to come out of the shell by my hand. But if I am going to eat cooked oysters, this is the way to eat them."

The idea for the recipe started when he was deer hunting in Montana and ate venison wrapped in bacon, breaded with Italian breadcrumbs, and broiled in the oven. Later that same year at a duck-hunting camp in Galliano, Louisiana, he and his friends were frying duck breasts. They had oysters to make a duck and oyster gumbo and someone suggested that they do oysters Montana-venison-style, but fried. So, they put it together.

Charlie Lieux enjoys a few raw oysters before cooking.

Tip: These oysters are crunchier than regular fried oysters and are great for introducing oysters to someone new to eating them.

1 pt. oysters
1 cup Italian breadcrumbs
1 lb. bacon, cut into thirds
2 cups milk
2-3 eggs
2 dashes Tabasco sauce
½ tsp. black pepper
⅓ tsp. garlic powder
½ tsp. Creole seasoning
1½ cups seasoned fish fry
Cooking oil for frying

Drain the oysters and roll them in breadcrumbs. Cut the bacon into 3-inch strips, wrap a strip around each oyster (like a saddle), and secure it with a round toothpick. Make an egg wash with milk, eggs, Tabasco sauce, black pepper, garlic powder, and Creole seasoning. Dip the bacon-wrapped oysters in the egg wash, and then roll in the fish fry. Fry at 350 degrees until the bacon is golden brown and the oysters float, no more than 5 minutes. Remove from oil and drain on paper towels. Serves 4.

Oyster Remoulade Po-boy

Tip: This is a very juicy sandwich so the oysters must be fried very crisp.

This jaw-stretcher from Oceana Grill in the New Orleans French Quarter is a fabulous take-off of the traditional oyster po-boy, south Louisiana's signature seafood sandwich. This award-winning preparation is unique. The remoulade sauce on coleslaw alone is one-of-a-kind. Add the delightful, sweet taste of the sautéed ripe peppers and you approach sublimity. The restaurant opened as a small ten-table affair in 2002 with the owner, Wassek Badr taking the orders and going back into the kitchen to cook it himself. In 2008, they cut a hole in the wall and expanded into the Olde N'awlins Cookery. In 2009 they opened the Jean Lafitte ballroom, also known as the Presidential Room, upstairs. Wassik's two sons are now the senior officers of a restaurant that can seat 350 patrons.

Remoulade Sauce

¼ cup fresh lemon juice
¾ cup vegetable oil
½ cup chopped onion
¼ cup chopped celery
2 tbsp. chopped garlic
2 tbsp. prepared horseradish
3 tbsp. Creole whole-grain mustard
3 tbsp. prepared yellow mustard
3 tbsp. ketchup
3 tbsp. chopped parsley
1 tsp. salt
¼ tsp. cayenne pepper
⅛ tsp. freshly ground black pepper

Blend all ingredients in a food processor. Use immediately or store in airtight container. Keeps about four days.

Oyster Remoulade Po-boy

1 cup white flour
1 cup corn flour
1 tbsp. parsley
1 tbsp. Tony Chachere's Original Creole Seasoning
1 tsp. garlic powder
32-40 oysters
Olive oil
1 clove garlic, minced
2 red bell peppers, julienned
2 yellow bell peppers, julienned
2 tbsp. butter
4 8-inch sections of French bread
Remoulade sauce
1 cup coleslaw
1 large tomato, sliced
1 red onion, thinly sliced
Sliced hamburger dill pickles

In a medium bowl, blend white flour, corn flour, parsley, Creole seasoning, and garlic powder. Roll oysters in flour mixture to coat evenly. Fry oysters in oil at 350 degrees until crispy and golden brown. Cover the bottom of a frying pan with olive oil. Add garlic and bell peppers and sauté until tender but not mushy. Slice open the French bread sections horizontally and lightly butter and toast the insides. Thickly spread remoulade sauce on both sides of the bread. On one half, lay coleslaw, sliced tomatoes, red onions, and pickle slices. On the other half, lay the crispy, fried oysters. Top plentifully with tender bell pepper strips. Fold halves together to eat. Serves 4.

Firecracker Oyster Po-boy

Have you ever had food explode in your mouth? This po-boy will do it. It goes three different ways at once with three pungent ingredients—oysters, blue cheese, and Thai chili sauce. But it all comes together with no single flavor dominating the others.

This extraordinary dish is served at Royal House Restaurant in the New Orleans French Quarter and was invented by then-executive chef Troy Robinson. The restaurant specializes in seafood and Creole cuisine. This dish was one of the winners in the po-boy contest at the 2010 Oyster Jubilee.

Tip: Many types of Thai chili sauces are available. For this dish, it is important to choose one with a honey base so that it sticks to the fried oysters. Thai chili sauces can be found in the International Section of any supermarket or in Asian food specialty stores.

Tip: Using expensive imported blue cheese is not necessary, but very cheap blue cheeses should also be avoided. The restaurant uses domestic Maytag Blue Cheese.

Tip: Spicy mayonnaise is simply mayonnaise blended with Louisiana Crystal Hot Sauce to taste.

Tip: This dish makes great appetizers when one fried, sauced oyster is placed per French bread round and sprinkled with blue cheese.

1½ pt. oysters
1 12-oz box dry shrimp fry
Cooking oil for frying
4 10-inch pieces French bread
1 pt. spicy mayonnaise
2 cups shredded lettuce
2 large tomatoes, sliced
12 dill pickle chips
1 cup Thai chili sauce
8 oz. blue cheese crumbles
Minced parsley for garnish
4 lemon wedges

Dredge oysters in shrimp fry breading. Fry in oil at 350 degrees for 2 minutes or until golden brown. While oysters are frying, slice open French bread horizontally and dress with spicy mayonnaise, lettuce, tomatoes, and pickles. After removing oysters from cooking oil, quickly toss with Thai chili sauce so that it will caramelize on the still-hot oysters. Place oysters on dressed French bread. Top with blue cheese crumbles while oysters are still warm so that the cheese slightly melts. Garnish with minced parsley and lemon wedges. Serves 4.

Oyster Cutlets

A cutlet is either a thin cut of meat or a patty of meat or fish that is breaded and then fried or broiled. These are patty-style cutlets. They look like oyster burgers and are crispy on the outside and mild and moist on the inside. Eat them plain or on a bun, dressed the way you wish.

2 cups chopped oysters, with liquor
2 tbsp. butter
2 tbsp. flour
Salt and pepper to taste
2 tbsp. lemon juice
6 eggs, divided
½ cup cracker crumbs, divided
Cooking oil for frying

Drain oysters; save the liquor and set it aside. Melt the butter in a medium saucepan. When it froths, add flour and stir to mix well. Add salt and pepper and the liquor from the oysters, and cook until thick. Remove from heat and add oysters and lemon juice. Add 4 well-beaten eggs. Return to fire and cook until thick. Add 4 tbsp. cracker crumbs, mix well, and spread on a platter to cool. When cool, shape into 4 cutlets. Dip cutlets into 2 well-beaten eggs, then dredge in ¼ cup cracker crumbs, and deep fry. Serves 4.

Seafood Muffulettas

Muffuletta sandwiches are unique to New Orleans, although their following elsewhere is growing. As created by Salvatore Lupo in 1906 at his Central Grocery on Decatur Street in the French Quarter, the sandwich was a 9-inch sesame-seeded muffuletta bun, sliced in half and layered with marinated olive salad, capicola, salami, mortadella, and mozzarella and provolone cheeses. But, in that seafood-crazed city, it was only a matter of time before someone started making seafood muffuletta sandwiches. Naturally, no two places do them alike. Here are two contrasting versions. Have fun!

Mr. Ed's Seafood Muffuletta

Mr. Ed's is a neighborhood restaurant on the edge of Bucktown, the old commercial fishing community on the Jefferson Parish side of the canal that separates it from New Orleans. It's where we ate our first seafood muffuletta. It was a lot different than what we expected. Their sandwich is built on a very large muffuletta bun, but the resemblance to the Central Grocery muffuletta ends there. It has no olive salad and no cheese.

"You don't need anything else, just garlic-buttered bread and seafood—and maybe some pickle chips," insists restaurant owner Ed McIntyre. Just the mention of adding olive salad to the sandwich causes him to shake his head violently (although he loves olive salad on the regular muffuletta). "Too much dressing messes it all up. This is almost like eating a seafood platter on a bun. You get the taste of all three."

Ed McIntyre with some of his restaurant's famous fried chicken.

6 4-oz. catfish fillets
1 cup yellow corn flour
¼ tsp. granulated garlic
1 tsp. salt
½ tsp. black pepper
4 dozen peeled shrimp
4 dozen oysters
Peanut oil for frying
2 tbsp. garlic butter
2 9-inch muffuletta loaves

Diagonally cut each catfish fillet into 3 strips and set aside. In a small bowl, mix corn flour, granulated garlic, salt, and pepper. Dredge shrimp, oysters, and catfish in the corn flour mixture, then fry in peanut oil at 350 degrees. When golden brown, remove from oil and drain on paper towels. Spread garlic butter on bread and toast in the oven at 350 degrees for about 2 minutes, until crispy. The sandwich is served with no other adornment unless you request otherwise. You may order it dressed with shredded iceberg lettuce, sliced tomatoes, pickles, and with mayonnaise or olive salad. Serves 4.

Pier 424 Seafood Muffuletta

This restaurant, located on Bourbon Street in the New Orleans French Quarter, is owned by three local brothers. Ninety percent of their menu is seafood, as the name of the eatery implies, and they are especially proud of their boiled seafood. This relatively new restaurant wants to do traditional New Orleans seafood dishes with an inspired spin, according to Carol Keltz, director of marketing and training. The sandwich has the basic components of a traditional muffuletta: olive salad, provolone cheese, and a smaller version of the big seeded bun. "We avoided catfish," says Carol, "because it is too plain. Oysters have more presence. Plus catfish doesn't hold up with olive salad and cheese. It gets mushy."

As for leaving out the olive salad, there was no chance of that. "The acidity and tartness of olives is a good compliment to seafood," says Carol. "There are combinations that you wouldn't think would work together. You try it and it's delicious. This is an amazing sandwich." She notes that it is important to toast the sandwich enough to melt the cheese, because it is a hot sandwich and the cheese needs to be incorporated with the fried seafood. "This sandwich is best," she says, "because it is not fancy. It is simple, with a burst of flavor."

1 egg
6 oz. buttermilk
1 tsp. lemon juice
8 oz. fish fry
1 tbsp. Creole seasoning
2 qt. cooking oil for frying
16 oysters
10 oz. peeled and deveined shrimp (50/60 count)
2 8-inch seeded muffuletta buns, sliced in half
8 slices Provolone cheese
4 oz. olive salad

Make an egg wash by blending the egg with buttermilk and lemon juice in a small bowl. In a separate bowl, mix fish fry and Creole seasoning. Heat oil in a heavy 4 qt. pot to 350 degrees. Dip oysters in egg wash, then dredge them in fish fry mixture, and shake off the excess. Heat cooking oil to 350 degrees and fry oysters for 2 minutes or until golden brown. Repeat the process with the shrimp. Place 2 slices Provolone cheese on each side of sliced buns. Heat the buns under a broiler for 2 minutes, or until cheese melts. Remove from heat. Top one side of each bun with olive salad. Top the other side with fried seafood. Put the two halves together to form a sandwich. Cut in half and serve with French fries or chips. Serves 4.

Timberton Tin Oysters

Joe Macaluso specializes in the evolving cooking style that is recognized as "Cajun Camp Cuisine." In south Louisiana, and to a lesser degree in north Louisiana, cooking is an anticipated activity at fishing, and most especially, hunting camps. That's where I learned to cook. The cook has an honored place in the social structure of the camp. He never has to get his own beer—just snap his fingers. And he never has to wash dishes!

Joe, the outdoors writer for the *Baton Rouge Advocate* newspaper is an avid hunter and fisherman. He is a member of the Timberton Social Club. "We hunt; we fish; we play *bourré*—whatever is in season." This dish is named after the camp and the tin muffin pans in which the dish is cooked and served.

Much of the mystique surrounding camp cuisine revolves around being original enough to make do with whatever is already at the camp. To leave the camp and go to civilization to get something needed is considered amateur. For this recipe, the hunters had a lot of oysters at the camp, but they were filled up with eating them raw. "I always liked Oysters Italiano but never had my own recipe," says Joe, "so I went looking through the pantry. We had green onions, garlic, dried herbs, and Progresso Bread Crumbs. This is what I did with them."

For some reason, every camp in Louisiana has a stack of metal muffin tins. I think people bring them to the camp when they get too much baked-on brown stain in the crevices. Timberton's supply came in handy. Joe serves the dish in the tins in which they were baked. "Hunters just eat 'em up," he says with a grin.

4 dozen oysters
8 strips bacon
2 sticks unsalted butter, divided
1 bunch green onions
2 pinches dried oregano
2 pinches dried basil
1 small pinch dried rosemary
Non-stick cooking spray
½ cup Italian breadcrumbs
¼ cup Parmesan/Romano cheese

Drain oysters and set aside. Fry bacon until crisp and set aside. Melt 1 stick of butter in a medium frying pan. Add green onions and sauté until they are tender and the edges are brown. Add oregano, basil, and rosemary and mix well. Melt 6 tbsp. butter and add to onion mixture. Stir in oysters and cook until the oysters firm up. Spray metal muffin tins with non-stick spray. Spoon oysters with sauce into the muffin cups. Crumble bacon and sprinkle on top of the oysters. Sprinkle 1 tsp. breadcrumbs in each cup, and top with ½ tsp. Parmesan/Romano cheese. Melt 2 tbsp. butter and drizzle over cheese. Bake at 350 degrees for 15-20 minutes. Serve in the muffin tins. Serves 4.

Broiled Oysters

Eva Vujnovich makes Tako toddies, while the krostula-crew works in the kitchen.

Eva Vujnovich of Belle Chasse, Louisiana, cooked this dish for Glenda and myself, as well as for the kitchen full of Croatian friends there to help her cook krostulas, the famous Dalmatian treat of fried and sugared sweet dough. The broiled oysters were so good it was hard to believe how simple the recipe was. Eva said that in the early days at the family oyster camp, cooking had to be simple, with simple ingredients.

Eva has had a long life in oysters. Her father was an oysterman and she lived at the oyster camp until age eight. "Daddy didn't care if I went to school, but Momma did. She pushed. We moved to Empire and I went to school there. I couldn't speak a word of English."

She married Pete Vujnovich, a dedicated oysterman, in 1954 and the family moved to New Orleans, where their six children were educated. In 1968, she began working in the family oyster shop, later known as Capt. Pete's Oysters on North Rampart Street in New Orleans. Eva worked there until Hurricane Katrina closed the shop permanently in 2005. "My job was pretty much anything. I shucked, delivered oysters all over town. I would do pretty much whatever anyone else didn't want to do, especially when Pete was on the boat."

My earliest memories of her are from the mid-1970s, standing over a perforated stainless steel skimming table, carefully and lovingly washing shucked oysters. She seldom spoke, but she saw everything.

4 dozen large oysters, drained
½ cup olive oil
10 cloves garlic, minced
4 tbsp. minced parsley
Salt and pepper to taste
2 lemons

Turn oven to broil. When hot, place oysters on a slotted grill pan so the water from the oysters can drain off as they cook. Broil 3-4 minutes. When the oysters are brown and the edges curl, turn them over and brown the other side. In a small pan, add olive oil, garlic, parsley, and salt and pepper. Sauté until the garlic is cooked, about 1 minute. Place browned oysters in a serving bowl and squeeze lemon juice over them. Drizzle the olive oil mixture over the oysters and serve with French bread. Serves 4.

Krostulas

The real action in Eva Vujnovich's kitchen started with the krostula preparation. Variously spelled kroštule, krustule, hrostula, and occasionally krostula, they are virtually an obsession with Dalmatian Croatians living in south Louisiana. Marija Vekic, says you can't have a Croatian wedding without krostulas. Domenica Cibilich explains that ten to fifteen women will get together to cook krostulas for the annual Plaquemines Parish Oyster Association supper dance. All present agree that making krostulas is too much work for one person, although one admits that it is also a good reason for friends to get together and visit.

Dough is mixed, rolled out, cut, tied in knots, fried, and spinkled with powder sugar. Reinforcements constantly arrive: Mary Jane Tesvich, Krsma Vojnovich, and Andrea Thibodeaux. Powdered sugar and chatter, much of it Croatian-fractured English, fills the air. Over it all, eighty-two-year-old Eva presides, supervising the krostula-making, leading discussions of the old ways at the camp, history, and family, and at one point preparing "Tako Toddies," a drink, made without ice or "fizz drinks," because none existed at oyster camps. "But we had whiskey, sugar, and lemons," she says with a grin.

The drink is simple, half of a cut-up lemon, mulled with three spoons of sugar in a glass, a big shot of whiskey, and some water. In later days when 7-Up became available, they used it instead of water.

After the krostulas were done, Eva broke out more food for everyone—broiled oysters, fried oysters, oyster soup, cheeses, pastrami, Tennessee country ham, hoghead cheese, black olives, green olives, onions, tomatoes, pickles, nuts, French bread, rolls, and sliced bread. It got quiet in the kitchen.

Making krostulas is a lot of work, but it is a good chance for family and friends to visit.

Tip: Kruškovac can be found in some liquor stores or better grocery stores. If not available, rum may be substituted.

6 large eggs
1 cup sugar
⅔ cup whiskey
3 tbsp. Kruškovac (a Croatian pear liqueur)
Pinch of salt
1 tsp. vanilla
4 tbsp. butter, softened
3 cups all purpose flour
Cooking oil for frying

Separate the eggs and beat the whites on high until stiff. In a separate bowl, mix egg yolks, sugar, whiskey, Kruškovac, salt, vanilla, and butter. Beat until the sugar melts, about 10-15 minutes. Add egg whites to yolk mixture and mix until blended. Reduce speed to low. Slowly add flour and continue to beat until a dough ball forms. Generously flour the counter and knead dough, adding flour as needed to keep the dough from sticking to the counter. Cut the dough into 3-inch balls, roll in flour to keep them from drying out, and set aside. Roll each ball as thin as possible. Cut into strips about an inch wide. The strips may be tied in knots or left in strips. Heat oil in a frying pan, drop strips of dough into pan, and fry until they just begin to brown. The krostulas will continue to brown after removal from the pan. Sprinkle with powdered sugar.

Oyster Kabobs

When Glenda and I first heard of this one, two thoughts crossed our mind. How do they keep the oysters on the skewers, and that doesn't sound very good. When John and Jane Tesvich of Nairn, Louisiana, prepared it for us, it knocked our socks off. Glenda fixed an eye on me and said, "We are going to do this at home."

1 pt. large oysters, drained, with liquor reserved
1 bell pepper, cut into 1½-inch squares
½ lb. smoked pork sausage, cut in ½-inch slices
1 medium onion, cut in 1-inch strips, separated into strips with 2-3 layers of onion
3 Roma tomatoes, cut in ½-inch slices

Heat the reserved oyster liquor and parboil the oysters in it until the oyster tips begin to curl. Remove oysters from pot and drain on paper towels. Thread the oysters onto skewers alternating with bell pepper, sausage, onion, and tomato slices. Baste with kabob sauce (recipe following).

Kabob Sauce
1 tsp. Tony Chachere's Original Creole Seasoning
4 tbsp. extra virgin olive oil
2 tbsp. red wine vinegar
Dash of garlic powder
2 tbsp. parmesan cheese

John Tesvich bastes his oyster kabobs frequently.

Tip: Use flat or double-pronged skewers to keep the oysters from spinning on the skewer.

Tip: The firm, meaty Roma tomatoes solve the problem of tomatoes turning to mush before the other food on the kabob cooks.

Place all ingredients in a small bowl and mix well. Heat grill and oil the grates with olive oil. Baste the kabobs with sauce, then place on grill, and cook until lightly browned, about 10 minutes. Baste the kabobs and then turn them over carefully to brown the other side. Use all of the sauce. Remove from grill and serve. Serves 4.

Oysters Jaubert

This superb recipe is from Bob Guertin who owned Guertin's Restaurant in New Orleans. In its short life, the restaurant was a cradle of culinary innovation. After trying this dish there, I begged and wheedled shamelessly to get the recipe. It's simple to fix, but tastes fabulous.

4 tbsp. butter
3 tbsp. flour
1½ cups milk
8 drops Tabasco sauce
1 tsp. salt
½ tsp. crushed tarragon
4 English muffins
8 slices Canadian bacon
16-24 fried oysters

Melt the butter in a saucepan. Gradually add flour, stirring constantly until smooth. Slowly add milk, stirring with a wire whisk. Simmer over low heat until sauce thickens. Add Tabasco sauce, salt, and tarragon and blend well. Keep the sauce warm on very low heat. Slice the English muffins in half and toast them. Place each muffin open-faced on a plate. Place a slice of Canadian bacon on each half. Top with 2-3 fried oysters. Spoon the sauce over the English muffins and serve. Serves 4.

Tip: This dish is good any time of day, but it is one of the few oyster dishes that is excellent for breakfast.

Jurisich's Boiled Oysters

Gently sloshing the boiling basket of oysters up and down a few times after the seasonings are added helps them to mix evenly.

Mitch Jurisich's seasoning package for boiled oysters.

Tip: It is very important to hose the oysters off under pressure to wash away any outside grit or it will end up inside the cooked oysters.

Tip: Mitch adds Ac'cent Flavor Enhancer whenever he boils any seafood. It is one of his secrets.

I tried this years ago, but I didn't have the secret. Mitch Jurisich, Jr. of Buras, Louisiana, showed me the secret. When I tried boiling them before, I followed the usual routine: add seasonings to the water, bring it to a boil, then add the seafood. The oysters came out completely unseasoned. Mitch showed me that the trick is to put the oysters and seasonings in cold water. Only after they are added is heat applied. His theory is that dropping oysters in boiling water causes them to react by clamping their shells shut tighter, preventing any seasoning from getting into the meat. His theory is that a gradual rise in water temperature causes the animals to relax their muscles, allowing seasoned water into the shells. Correct or not—his way works like a charm. They are delicious. "I take these to football tailgate parties," says Mitch. "I get a bigger turnout for these than for charbroiled oysters."

Mitch and his brother Frank are part of the third generation of an oyster-fishing family that is very likely to run into four generations. His son Nathan is very interested in the business, but Mitch told him he had to get more schooling first. Currently, he works on the boat part time and in summers. "As for the future of oystering, there will be some bumps in the road. Our harvests will become smaller, both because of coastal erosion and because of coastal restoration done the wrong way. But, I'm optimistic."

¾ **bushel live oysters (half sack)**
1 **26-oz. box salt**
1 **64-oz. jar Cajun Land Complete Crab, Shrimp, and Crawfish Boil**
1 **4-oz. bottle liquid crab boil**
1 **6-oz. bottle Crystal hot sauce**
2 **3-oz. can Ac'cent Flavor Enhancer**
1 **5½-oz. jar granulated garlic**

Wash oysters with a hose until cleaned thoroughly. Put cleaned oysters in an 80-quart boiling pot. Add enough cold tap water to cover the oysters. Add all the seasonings and bring to a boil. Once the water begins to boil, cook for 10 minutes. Turn off the heat and allow the oysters to soak for 20 minutes, then start sampling for seasoning.

When the seasoning is to your taste, remove the oysters from the water and drain. Serves 6.

Hangtown Fry

Pansy Bray, a food writer from Hoquiam, Washington, clued me in to this recipe, a west coast classic, in 1997. The Bray family has good seafood credentials. Her father was a commercial fisherman and seafood processor. Her former husband Lester is a commercial fisherman, as are sons Ricky, Terry, and Russell, who are salmon gillnetters in Cordova, Alaska.

The recipe comes from a high, California mountain mining town called Hangtown. The august village received its name from the number of desperadoes they strung up there. The town today is listed as Placerville, California, because some of the city fathers felt that Hangtown wasn't really a name that would attract newcomers.

The story goes that a prospector up in the hills struck it rich, and when he came to town, he went to the saloon of the El Dorado Hotel and asked what the most expensive dish in the house was. When he was told that oysters were, he ordered a pan of them, with eight or ten eggs mixed up, and garnished with strips of bacon. This dish became known as "Hangtown Fry." We cook it both for main meals and breakfasts. It's good anytime.

9 eggs, divided
2 tbsp. cream, divided
1 pt. oysters, drained
¾ cup flour
¾ cup seasoned breadcrumbs
6 slices bacon
Cooking oil for frying
Salt and pepper

Beat 1 egg with 1 tbsp. cream. Dip the oysters in flour, then in the egg wash, then in the breadcrumbs, and set aside. Fry the bacon until crisp, remove the bacon, and put it on a paper towel to drain. Reserve the bacon drippings for later. Fry the oysters in oil until brown and crisp. Drain the oysters on paper towels. Beat 8 eggs with 1 tbsp. cream. Add salt and pepper to taste. Pour ¼ of the egg mixture into 1 tbsp. bacon drippings and cook on low heat. When the eggs are done, place on a plate. Garnish with bacon and fried oysters. Repeat the process three more times until the eggs are done. Serves 4.

Frizzled Oysters

Frizzling can be defined as scorching or searing with heat, as well as heating something enough to make it curl. In this dish, the breadcrumbs are certainly browned, but neither the breadcrumbs nor the oysters can be described as being scorched or seared. Nevertheless, frizzled oyster recipes are common and all of them are basically variations of the same thing. This is "down home" cooking. When washed oysters with very little salt are used, the amount of salt may need to be increased. This dish really showcases the taste of oysters.

5 tbsp. butter
3 eggs, beaten
1 cup dried breadcrumbs
1 pt. oysters, with liquor
½ tsp. salt
½ tsp. pepper
¼ tsp. dried mustard

Melt the butter in a frying pan over medium heat. While the butter is melting, mix together the eggs and breadcrumbs. When the butter has melted and is starting to sizzle, add the egg and breadcrumb mixture. Stir once, then add the oysters and their liquor. Add salt, pepper, and mustard. Mix oysters into the breadcrumbs. Cook for 7-10 minutes, stirring and turning the mix over when the bottom becomes browned. Serves 4.

Mary Poe's Oyster Stew

Mary's father, Major Newlin, shown standing at the door of his camp, was a major influence on her love of cooking and the outdoors.

Tip: Do not boil this dish. Mary says that the only way to ruin this "very, very simple dish" is to boil it.

Tip: Do not cook the onions and celery until they are mushy, as is so often done with the holy trinity of seasonings. In this dish, their slight resistance to the tooth is delightful.

Mary and Jeff Poe are charter fishing guides who live on the shores of Calcasieu Lake. Although Mary is famous for her fishing ability, her culinary skills are just as impressive. During the winter months, Jeff and the Poe's son Nick guide waterfowl hunters, while Mary prepares feasts for the hunters staying in their lodge. Often, oyster stew is on the menu, served immediately before the entrée. "A lot of duck hunters love oysters," she explains. Mary credits the dish to her father, Major Newlin, who according to Mary loved to cook as much as he loved to fish. "He cooked every day until the day he died. He absolutely loved cooking."

1 stick butter
1½ cups chopped onions
1 cup chopped celery
1 tbsp. flour
1 pt. oysters, drained
1 cup oyster liquor
1 cup half-and-half
Salt and pepper to taste
1 tbsp. parsley

Melt the butter, add onions and celery, and sauté until the onions are tender. Stir in flour and mix until blended. Add oysters and cook about 5 minutes until the oysters' edges curl. Pour in the oyster liquor (if you don't have enough liquor to make a cup, add either water or half-and-half). Simmer for 15 minutes. Reduce the heat to low and slowly add the cup of half-and-half, stirring constantly. Be careful not to boil the half-and-half. Season to taste with salt and pepper. Sprinkle in the parsley. Cook only enough for the seasonings to meld, about 1 minute. Serves 4.

Golden Oyster Stew

Is it a soup or is it a stew? I dunno, but this delightful, cheesy dish sticks to the ribs and is good. A *Lagniappe* newsletter reader sent the recipe to us in 2000. Then in February 2007, *Southern Living* magazine printed a very similar recipe under the same name. Since then, versions of the recipe have popped up all over the internet.

½ cup chopped onion
½ cup chopped celery
¼ cup butter
2 cups sliced mushrooms
¼ cup flour
1 tsp. salt
½ tsp. black pepper
2 cups milk
1½ cups grated sharp cheddar cheese
1 pt. oysters
1 10½-oz. can cream of potato soup
1 2-oz. jar diced pimentos
¼ tsp. hot sauce

Sauté onions and celery in butter until tender. Add mushrooms and cook until tender, about 5 minutes. Over low heat, stir flour, salt, and pepper into mixture. Add milk and stir until thickened. Add cheese and stir until melted. Add oysters, soup, pimentos, and hot sauce. Heat for 10 minutes, or until oysters begin to curl. Serves 4.

Tip: If the oysters are large, you may want to cut them up, because you want at least a piece of oyster in every spoonful.

Louisiana Oyster Curry

Tip: Don't leave out the chopped sour apple in this dish. The best curries have a hint of fruit. We use a granny smith apple.

Curries are one of our favorite ways of preparing seafood, and although shrimp are our usual victims, oysters work well, too. Curry powder, as purchased off the shelf, makes British curries. About twenty different ingredients go into British curry powders so the variations are endless. If you don't like one brand, try another. Some of the ingredients in curry powders have a short shelf life, so this is one spice best rotated often.

2 tsp. curry powder
2 tsp. flour
2 cups cream
3 tbsp. minced onion
5 tbsp. chopped sour apple
1 qt. oysters, drained
Lemon juice
Creole seasoning
Cooked rice

Blend together curry powder and flour in a medium saucepan. Add cream, onion, and sour apple. Bring to a boil and simmer 20 minutes. Add oysters to the sauce and cook until the edges of the oysters curl. Remove from heat and add a squirt of lemon juice. Season to taste with Creole seasoning. Serve with cooked rice. Serves 4.

Oysters in Brown Sauce

This is an "old timey" recipe that is still as good as it ever was. Brown sauces, of course, have a roux. This recipe uses a blonde one, but it's still a roux. The finished dish has a sauce too thick to put over rice, but it is good served over a toasted English muffin or with freshly baked bread.

1 pt. oysters, with liquor
1 medium carrot, finely chopped
¼ cup finely chopped onion
¼ cup finely chopped parsley
4 tbsp. butter
2 tbsp. flour
1 rounded tsp. beef bouillon granules
1 cup cream
1 egg yolk, beaten
1 tsp. lemon juice
Salt and pepper

Scald the oysters in their own liquor. Drain the oysters and save the liquor. Fry carrot, onion, and parsley in butter until tender. Add flour and cook until lightly browned. Add oyster liquor and beef bouillon. Simmer until thick, stirring constantly. Add oysters, cream, and beaten egg yolk. Reheat lightly and remove from fire. Add lemon juice and salt and pepper to taste. Serve immediately. Serves 3-4.

Brown Gravy Oyster Spaghetti

This dish has a rich, delicious, mushroom-accented brown sauce. The gravy would work with a beef stew, but it is also perfect here. It is so different than other oyster spaghettis. Some are tomato-based, some are cream-based, others are built around olive oil or butter, but a brown spaghetti sauce is unusual. It was created by Larry Roussel of Hester, Louisiana, a self-trained cooking prodigy. He describes himself as a "Chook," explaining, "I'm not a chef; I'm not a cook; I'm somewhere between; I'm a self-proclaimed Chook." Larry cooks weekly on ABC 26, WGNO television in New Orleans, as "Uncle Larry" and his recipes appear under that name on the WGNO Web site. Larry was a frequent contributor to my *Lagniappe* fisheries newsletter. This dish is both "down-home" and "up town" at the same time. You will sop up every bit of the gravy with bread—I promise!

1 qt. oysters, with liquor
¼ cup cooking oil
2 medium onions, chopped
1 bell pepper, chopped
2 stalks celery, chopped
½ cup flour
1 10-oz. can Ro*tel Tomato and Green Chilies
1 6½-oz. can mushroom stems and pieces
1 10¾-oz. can cream of mushroom soup
1 10¾-oz. can cream of celery soup
4 cups water
4 tbsp. Kitchen Bouquet
1 tsp. Creole seasoning
2 tsp. salt
1 tsp. black pepper
1 tsp. garlic powder
1 heaping tbsp. dried parsley flakes
1 lb. spaghetti

Strain oyster liquor from oysters, save liquor, and set both aside. Combine oil, onions, bell pepper, and celery in a large pot. Sauté for 5 minutes. Add flour and stir into seasoning. Add tomatoes, mushrooms, mushroom soup, and celery soup. Add oyster liquor and sauté for 5 minutes. Add water and bring to a boil, then add Kitchen Bouquet, Creole seasoning, salt, black pepper, garlic powder, and parsley flakes. Add oysters and cook uncovered for 20-30 minutes. Prepare spaghetti according to package directions while sauce cooks. Serves 8.

Croatian-Style Fishermen's Oyster Spaghetti

This is the classic savory dish of the Croatian community in southeast Louisiana. Croatia is just a hop across the Adriatic Sea from Italy, so pastas are naturally the starch of choice in their diets. Only after coming to Louisiana did they learn to eat rice. John Tesvich, with help from his wife Jane, cooked this great dish for us. Both are pedigreed Croatians and their story is illustrative of the journeys of Louisiana's Croatians. Jane's parents, Andrew and Kate Pobrica, were born in Croatia. Grandfather Lawrence Pobrica was an oysterman. Her father didn't enter the oyster business; instead, he became a businessman in Plaquemines Parish.

John's family history in the U.S. goes back further. One maternal great-grandfather, Ante Pausina, died in the 1893 Hurricane while fishing oysters near the now-gone camp settlement of Salt Works (Salina in Croatian) in Plaquemines Parish. On his father's side, Ivo Tesvich immigrated to Louisiana from Donja Vrućica in the late 1800s. After working several years, he returned to Croatia, got married, and returned with his bride to his oyster camp in Salina. He retired comfortably to Croatia, by then part of Yugoslavia, in 1927 or 1928, but sent his eldest son Kuzma back to Louisiana to work in the oyster business in 1929. Younger brother, Ante, known as "Tony," followed in 1931 at the age of sixteen. Tony was John's father.

The country was in the midst of the Great Depression and oysters were difficult to sell. The brothers worked for other oystermen and lived on Bayou Chalon, almost as subsistence fishermen. Nevertheless, they scraped together $1,200 in savings, which they used to build a camp on Bayou Robinson. Then they borrowed $5,000, a huge sum in those days, from uncles and a friend to buy a lugger boat. They were finally in business for themselves. Even though oyster dredges had not yet been invented and every oyster had to be hand-tonged, they paid for the boat in the first year.

Tony was drafted into the United States Army for four years during World War II. In 1954, he returned to Yugoslavia, where he met and married a Croatian girl, Tereza Juričević. John's parents moved from the Bayou Robinson camp to Port Sulphur before his birth in 1957,

The oyster camps of Tony and Kuzma Tesvich on Bayou Robinson were impressive. Tony's camp, in the foreground with two cypress cisterns, had peach and fig trees, grape trellises, and a vegetable garden, 1956. (Courtesy Domenica Cibilich and John Tesvich)

Left to right, "Captain John" Zaninovich, "Pistol" Granich, and "Ante" Tony Tesvich on the porch of Zaninovich's Bayou Robinson camp, ca. 1975. Photo by Mrs. James Hoffman. (Courtesy John Tesvich)

but John maintains that he grew up at the camp. "We spent all our time there when not in school."

After graduating from the University of New Orleans with a degree in mechanical engineering, he met Jane at a Plaquemines Parish Oyster Association supper dance in 1978 and married her in 1980. John worked a stint as an engineer but quit in 1982 to return to the oyster business. "I was the oldest boy and expected to carry on the family business."

With brother-in-law Luke Cibilich, John has expanded the business and branched off on his own with more leases and boats, as well as operating with partner Patrick Fahey, AmeriPure Inc., an oyster processing plant.

John says that he learned to cook on the oyster boat by watching his dad. "My dad always cooked. We never had sandwiches. My mom learned to cook from my dad and cooked every day. Dad didn't like leftovers—didn't believe in them. We had two German shepherds. We ate hearty, fresh-cooked food. We had red bean soup," he says with a grin.

"I never ate a cream-based white oyster sauce until I left home. Croatians always eat tomato-based sauce." As for why spaghetti is so common, John says, "We ate what we had on the boat. We didn't have refrigeration or meat. Believe it or not, Croatians eat pasta with bread. Croatians always know where to find the best bread."

Jane compliments husband John on his cooking.

Tip: John stresses that cooking the tomato sauce for at least 45 minutes is critical to turn the taste from a "raw sour tomato taste to a rich, thick brownish sauce."

Tip: Add the oysters late to this dish so the sauce won't be diluted and the oysters overcooked. The oysters add additional liquid to the sauce. John says if you want a meatless Lenten dish, just delete the bacon and it will still be good.

1 qt. oysters, with liquor
3 slices bacon, chopped
3 tbsp. olive oil
4 cups chopped onions
1 stalk celery, chopped
½ bell pepper, chopped
6 cloves garlic, minced and divided
2 8-oz. cans tomato sauce
1 6-oz. can tomato paste
3 bay leaves
Salt and pepper to taste
¼ cup chopped parsley
Pasta of your choice

Drain the oysters and reserve the liquor. Heat the liquor to boiling and add the oysters. Parboil them until the edges curl. Remove oysters from pot and drain on paper towels. Save the liquor. In a separate pan, brown the bacon and then add olive oil, onions, celery, bell pepper, and half of the garlic. Sauté until vegetables are tender. Stir in tomato sauce and tomato paste. Add in 1½ cups oyster liquor and bay leaves and simmer on low heat for 45 minutes. If you don't have enough liquor, add water to make up the difference. Stir often to prevent burning as the sauce thickens. Add additional liquor as required. Stir in oysters, salt and pepper, parsley, and remaining garlic. Sauté an additional 15 minutes, stirring occasionally. Turn off the fire and let the sauce sit for 20 minutes to blend flavors. Serve over pasta. Serves 4-6.

Oyster Tasso Pasta

This recipe is from Melissa Cibilich of Plaquemines Parish. Melissa is Croatian, but this isn't a Croatian spaghetti; Croatian spaghetti is always red. What it is, is just wonderful. It is creamy, mild, and delicate. Melissa won a 4-H Seafood Cooking Contest with it. I was fortunate enough to be a judge and I have saved the recipe for sixteen years. Tasso, for those unfamiliar with it, is lean, heavily smoked pork shoulder that is used as seasoning in Cajun Country. It is available everywhere in south Louisiana, in gourmet shops, and on the Internet elsewhere.

1 stick butter
1 small onion, chopped
1 bunch green onions, chopped
4 oz. tasso, cut into ½-inch pieces
1 pt. oysters, drained
Salt and pepper to taste
1 pt. whipping cream
4 tbsp. grated Romano cheese
1 tbsp. chopped parsley
8 oz. thin pasta

Melt the butter in a large skillet. Add onion, green onions, and tasso. Sauté until onion and green onions are transparent. Add drained oysters and salt and pepper. Cook on medium heat for 5 minutes, then add whipping cream. Cook an additional minute. Remove from heat and stir in cheese and parsley. In a separate pot, cook pasta according to package directions. Stir the drained pasta into the oyster mixture and mix well. Serves 6-8.

Oysters Bordelaise

Tip: Be sure to add the full amount of garlic. John says the surest way to "mess up" this dish is to not use enough garlic.

Tip: If the pasta is too dry, drizzle a little olive oil over it before serving.

John Supan, a Louisiana State University professor and the university's resident oyster expert, shared this dish with us at his rural St. Tammany Parish home. He called it a classic French dish, not a Cajun dish—not one to use hot sauce with, because it would overwhelm the recipe's delicate taste. According to John, a bordelaise sauce is simply one made with olive oil, garlic, green onions, and bay leaves.

Reference sources typically describe bordelaise sauces as being made with red wine and some source of beef flavoring—bone marrow, beef or veal stock, beef broth, consommé, or bouillon. However the *Saveur* magazine Web site makes allowance for a "Creole bordelaise" which is indeed made with oil, garlic, and green onions. New Orleans food expert Tom Fitzmorris agrees.

John describes this as a family recipe of Sylvester Pagano, a part-time Mississippi oysterman whose sister owned Annie's Restaurant, a famous Pass Christian restaurant that succumbed to Hurricane Katrina. Pagano, who usually tonged on Square Handkerchief Reef, knew that the best quality oysters grew off-bottom, so he would use a piling scraper to scrape them loose from bridge pilings and then retrieve them with tongs.

⅓ cup olive oil
3 green onions, chopped and separated into tops and bottoms
1 qt. oysters, drained
1 bay leaf
3 tbsp. crushed garlic
12 oz. vermicelli
1-inch slice lemon
Salt to taste
Parmesan cheese
French bread

Cover the bottom of a large skillet with olive oil. Add onion bottoms and sauté until tender. Add oysters, bay leaf, and garlic and sauté until oyster edges curl. While the oysters are cooking, prepare vermicelli according to package directions. Squeeze juice from lemon, add juice and lemon to oyster mixture, and stir. Cook 5 minutes. Salt to taste and remove from heat. Combine oyster mixture and green onion tops with cooked, drained pasta. Mix well, then cover and let sit for ten minutes while flavors meld. Remix, then serve with Parmesan cheese to taste and hot French bread. Serves 4-6.

Oyster Fricassee

Tip: If the oysters were shucked at home and are saltier than washed oysters, the salt in the recipe should be reduced to ¼ tsp.

In south Louisiana, chickens or rabbits are the usual victims in a fricassee. This is close to a classical fricassee. A meat (in this case oysters) is sautéed in butter, then slowly cooked or stewed in a sauce with or without veggies until the meat is tender and the sauce is thick. Oyster fricassees almost always use egg yolks. Another difference between an oyster fricassee and chicken or rabbit is that an oyster fricassee is best served on toast points rather than rice.

1 qt. oysters
2 tbsp. butter
1 tbsp. flour
½ tsp. salt
¼ tsp. black pepper
¼ tsp. grated nutmeg
3 egg yolks, beaten
3 tbsp. olive oil
1 tbsp. lemon juice
1 tbsp. finely minced parsley

Strain liquor from oysters and set both liquor and oysters aside. Heat butter in a saucepan over medium-low heat until it barely froths. Add flour and stir constantly, until it becomes golden brown in color. Add oyster liquor and cook uncovered until it thickens. Add salt, pepper, and nutmeg. Reduce heat to medium-low, add oysters, and cook until the edges of the oysters curl. Add egg yolks, olive oil, and lemon juice. Cook until thickened, stirring occasionally. Add parsley and serve over toast points. Serves 4-6.

Jenna's Oyster Étouffée

Frank Jurisich is an oysterman. This recipe is named after his daughter. Jenna's main interest in oysters now is eating them. Her sixteen-year-old brother, Frank Joseph Jurisich, Jr., is looking forward to the day that he can work the family oyster beds with his father. Frank's wife Sissy produced the recipe, but he doesn't know where she got the idea. He thinks that it is a spin-off of a crawfish étoufée recipe. "It's quick; it's easy; it winds up being good, so its win, win, win," he says, adding, "I cook this at the hunting camp for Alabama friends. They can't pronounce it, but they really love it. One called it 'oopa-loopa-toopa something.'"

1 qt. oysters
1 cup chopped onion
1 cup chopped bell pepper
1 cup chopped celery
1 stick unsalted butter
2 cans cream of celery soup
2 tbsp. Creole seasoning or less if oysters are salty
1 lb. angel hair pasta

Drain oysters and set aside. Sauté onion, bell pepper, and celery in butter until tender. Add cream of celery soup and Creole seasoning. Cook over medium heat for 15 minutes, stirring frequently. Add oysters and cook until oysters are firm and their edges curl, about 15-20 minutes. Serve over pasta prepared according to package directions. Serves 4-6.

Frank Jurisich peeks mischievously through the steam rising from the camp cook stove.

Tip: If you prefer to eat étouffée the typical Cajun way, this dish can also be served over rice.

"It Was Really Like Slave Labor"

Eighty-year old Mitchell B. "Pop" Jurisich, Sr. watched as son Frank worked over the stove in the camp at the family's boat dock. He talked about his life as a Plaquemines Parish oysterman. "I started work when I was thirteen years old and I worked with oysters until I was seventy years old. Now, when the weather is good, I still go out with a small Lafitte skiff to check things out."

The family has history in the business. Pop's father Frank Jurisich was born in Croatia in 1889. At the tender age of thirteen, he left his home country for Louisiana. Croatians had been emigrating from their country to the state in significant numbers for more than fifty years. Young Frank entered during a period of peak immigration. "As soon as he got here," says Pop, "he went by train to Empire and the sponsor who paid for his trip put him to work on an oyster boat."

Sponsors were typically fellow countrymen, often relatives, who were already established in the United States and needed labor for their oyster businesses. The lad worked for five years for only food and clothes to pay off the debt he owed for transportation to the new country. Only after that could he begin to work for wages and save money for his own future.

In his late twenties, Frank got his own boat. Then he began to acquire oyster leases. The oldest Jurisich family lease is in Bayou La Chute and dates back to 1920. It is still in the family today and is being worked by Pop's sons, forty-seven-year-old Mitch Jr., and forty-six-year-old Frank, both full-time oystermen. The family now cultivates "a little more than 14,000 acres of leases," and operates three boats.

Pop shows great passion as he talks. His alert brown eyes are intense and he is articulate.

"I have seen plenty changes—plenty.

"Now we do everything with [oyster] dredges. We used to have to use rakes; Frenchmen called them oyster tongs. We used to have to shovel seed [oysters] by hand to plant them. Now they use high-pressure hoses.

Mitch Jurisich, Sr. shucks oysters with his sons, Frank (left) and Mitch, Jr. (right).

"It was a back-breaking job. We used to hand-tong the oysters into a small flatboat. Then we would pole the boat to a hard reef made of shell hash. We got the shell hash from beaches. We would use a shovel and wheelbarrow to load the big boat, a gasoline-powered lugger. Then we would run to the reef and spread the shell hash from the big boat onto the reef with shovels. It was hard work.

"Anyway, we would cull the oysters in the small boats by hand. The singles [oysters broken from clusters] would go overboard so the shells could get clean and accumulate until we had one hundred or so sacks—whatever the order was. Then we would rake them up again into the flatboat and put them into baskets for sacking.

"The empty shells from the culling would be taken with the flatboat to land to be piled up to dry and clean-up. We replanted those shells on the reefs in the summer to catch spat.

"After the oysters were sacked, we would take them to the big boat and after they were loaded on it, we would go to Empire. The oyster sacks were unloaded by hand—no conveyors—to a truck.

"The business is so easy now. When I got into it, it was really like slave labor."

Not all of Pop's memories are about oysters. His brow furrows and he frowns when he talks about the changes to Louisiana's marshes.

Mitch's father Frank stands nearest the center door of the family camp on Bayou La Chute. Mitch's mother, Neda stands in the doorway on the left with Mitch as a toddler at her feet and blonde-haired daughter Eva under her arm. Notice the lack of screens. They were put up for sleeping every evening and removed every morning. (Courtesy Eva Vujnovich)

Oystering was hard work. Every oyster had to be tonged with tongs (rakes) like those on the side of the boat behind the seated man, then culled by hand and either bedded with shovels or shoveled into sacks for sale (left to right, Johnny Murina, unknown, Anthony Tesvich). (Courtesy Ralph "Buddy" Pausina)

"When they started digging deepwater canals, Empire to the Gulf, or to Lafitte. . . . Our politicians were trying to help us. The original canals were to make navigation easier for us and others. A lot of the bayous were very shallow.

"It changed all the tides. The canals took the tides from the natural bayous. It hurt oyster growth and by the mid-1940s I began to see coastal erosion. Most wouldn't see it, but I lived there and I saw. Heavy boat traffic widened the canals. That was followed by oil rigs and then pipelines."

He sits quietly for a long while, then looks out the camp window before speaking. "The future? My kids will be able to finish their careers, but my grandkids—I don't know."

Frank, who has been listening quietly, peers through the steam coming off his pasta pot. He's more sanguine. "Oysters will be here in some fashion—even with coastal erosion. Unless political intervention stops us. Our problems are more man-made than natural."

Pop doesn't reply. But he smiles faintly.

Dredging, first for navigation and later for oil production, changed the face and ecology of coastal Louisiana. Photo is pre-1928 on Bayou Teche. (Courtesy Iberia Parish Library)

Oysters Creole

This is one of the oldest recipes collected and printed in the *Lagniappe* newsletter, dating back to 1977. Most Creole recipes are shrimp Creoles, but even the origin of the preparation of shrimp Creole is shrouded in obscurity. One thing that all Creoles have in common is that they are red, made with a dominant dose of tomato products—sauce, paste, canned, fresh, or stewed. This one is a little odd because it uses tomato juice. It's tasty and it doesn't have a tomato bite.

1 pt. oysters
3 tbsp. chopped onion
2 tbsp. butter
3 tbsp. flour
1 cup tomato juice
2 tbsp. chopped parsley
¼ tsp. Tabasco sauce
¾ tsp. salt
Buttered toast

Drain oysters. Cook onion in butter until tender. Blend in flour, add tomato juice, and cook until thick, stirring constantly. Add oysters, parsley, Tabasco sauce, and salt and simmer about 5 minutes, or until the oyster edges begin to curl. Serve on toast. Serves 4.

Oysters in a Pan

Tip: The chicken stock must be warm, because using cold liquid when thickening the roux will ruin the bond between the flour and the water.

Outdoor writer Jeff Bruhl, of Madisonville, Louisiana, sent this recipe to us, claiming that he got it from a friend in Kentucky. I don't know where his friend got the recipe, but it has New Orleans Creole written all over it. A dense, home-made potato bread is perfect to serve the dish on because it has the character to stand up to the rich sauce. This recipe has 4-star taste!

1 stick butter
1 cup chopped onion
½ cup chopped bell pepper
1 tbsp. chopped garlic
1 cup chopped green onions
¼ cup chopped celery
1 qt. oysters
1 tbsp. Creole seasoning
2 tbsp. Worcestershire sauce
1 tbsp. hot sauce
¼ cup flour
1 cup warm chicken stock
Toasted bread

Melt butter in a large cast-iron pan. Add onions, bell pepper, garlic, green onions, and celery and sauté the vegetables until tender. Add oysters and cook on medium-high heat until the edges curl. Add Creole seasoning, Worcestershire sauce, and hot sauce. Add flour slowly, stirring to mix while adding. Simmer until thickened. Slowly add chicken stock until gravy is formed. Continue cooking until desired thickness is reached. Serve over toasted bread. Serves 4.

Clubhouse Oysters

This recipe is interesting. We like to collect old recipes and this one was hand-written with no reference to who created it. An Internet search, at least under this name, produced zilch. The reason that the recipe is odd is that it is impossible to get 1½ cups of oyster liquor out of a pint of oysters—even if you wrung them. We keep extra oyster liquor in the freezer for just such circumstances, but we have found that with this recipe, if you don't have enough liquor you can add water to make up the difference. This one is good, with a mustard taste that is tangy but doesn't overwhelm the oysters.

1 pt. oysters, with liquor
3 tbsp. butter
4 tbsp. flour
1½ tsp. prepared mustard
½ tsp. paprika
1 tsp. parsley
1 tsp. salt
1½ cups oyster liquor
2 tbsp. lemon juice
2 tbsp. Worcestershire sauce
Toasted bread

Drain the oysters, save the liquor, and set aside. Melt the butter in a medium saucepan and add the flour. Mix well to blend. Add mustard, paprika, parsley, salt, and oyster liquor. Simmer uncovered until the sauce thickens slightly. Add lemon juice, Worcestershire sauce, and oysters. Simmer uncovered, stirring occasionally, until the oysters become firm and the edges of the oysters curl. If the sauce is too thin to put over toast, simmer slightly longer. Serve over toasted bread. Serves 4.

Oysters Noon

This recipe promised to be a lot of fun—and it was. Ann Taylor of Luling, Louisiana, said that she was going to cook her mother's "absolute favorite oyster recipe in the world" for us. Ann's mother, Colette Lottinger, writes a monthly cooking column in the *Louisiana Sportsman* magazine and produced the cookbook *How Sportsmen Cook* based on recipes in the column, as well as her own. Colette had obtained the recipe from the late Johnny Hoffman, the truly great Cajun humorist from Thibodaux, Louisiana. Many of Hoffmann's jokes revolved around the adventures of his *Oncle Noon* and *Tante Mess* in the fictitious town of Barricade, Louisiana. Hoffmann entered this recipe in the 1977 Bayou Gourmet Cookbook Contest in Houma and won both Grand Prize and First Place in the Seafood Category.

Both Ann and Colette cooked, but the real wheel horse in the kitchen was Ann's father Allen Lottinger, who in real life is still involved in the family's publishing businesses. Tony, Ann's husband, who is the publisher of the *Louisiana Sportsman* and was chief oyster opener of the day, explained that Oysters Noon was the first meal that Ann ever cooked for him after he met her at LSU. "Then they took me to Grand Isle. They had a camp on the beach. I figured that if I got married to her, they would take me to the camp some more." Ann, for her part, is an outdoors photographer, the editorial director of the *St. Charles Herald Guide* newspaper, and in 2009 was appointed to the Louisiana Wildlife and Fisheries Commission.

Allen Lottinger pitched in to do much of the cooking for daughter Ann.

Tip: This recipe should be prepared in a cast iron skillet, both to cook it properly and for presentation.

1 qt. oysters, drained
8 slices bacon
1 stick butter
1 cup finely chopped green onions
2 cups sliced mushrooms
2 tbsp. Pickapeppa sauce
½ tsp. Tabasco sauce
2 cups breadcrumbs
8 oz. grated cheddar cheese
⅓ cup chopped parsley

Pat the oysters dry with paper towels, and set aside. Fry bacon until crisp in a large, cast-iron skillet. Remove bacon from pan and set aside. Drain drippings from skillet. Add butter to skillet and melt over medium heat. Add green onions and cook until soft. Stir in mushrooms and sauté 3-4 more minutes. Add Pickapeppa sauce, Tabasco sauce, and oysters. Sauté until the oysters begin to curl. Remove from heat, crumble bacon, and scatter it over the pan. Sprinkle with breadcrumbs and grated cheese. Bake in a preheated 350 degree oven for 15 minutes or until the cheese is bubbly. Sprinkle with chopped parsley and serve in the skillet. Serves 4-6.

Alario's Oyster Mosca

"Our family," says Eva Alario Corcoran, "eats at Mosca's Restaurant at least twice a month. I have been going there since I was a little girl. We always order the same thing: Italian Crab Salad, Spaghetti and Bordelaise, Bean Soup, Shrimp or Oyster Mosca, Chicken a la Grande, then Pineapple Fluff for desert and then finally a shot of Nocello." It is traditional to share entrées in this stubbornly independent restaurant located between Westwego and Avondale, Louisiana.

Eva, who with her sister, Kathy Alario Choquette, and aunt, Barbara Alario Ballas, runs the family business, Alario Bros. Hardware & Fisherman Supplies in Westwego, cooks a lot. "I like to cook on my terms. Who wants to work all day and come home and cook? But I do like to cook hard dishes—challenging dishes." This recipe, she says is as close as she can come to the original dish at Mosca's. We thought it was better!

Eva Alario Corcoran says that her three sons keep her working like a short order cook.

Tip: Eva calls oyster liquor "gold" and says that she and her mother Bebe Alario freeze any surplus they have for later use.

Tip: Eva says she never takes her hand off the oven door during the broiling process, because it is easy to burn the dish if not watched closely.

1 pt. oysters, with liquor
3 tbsp. extra virgin olive oil
3 tbsp. minced garlic
½ tsp. dried rosemary
2 cups Italian breadcrumbs
½ cup + 2 tbsp. Parmesan cheese
Juice of ½ lemon

Preheat oven to 400 degrees. Drain the oysters, and reserve the liquor. In a pan, add olive oil and garlic. Sauté until the garlic is well done. Be careful not to burn the garlic. Add the rosemary and ½ cup oyster liquor. Add the oysters and cook until the edges of the oysters curl. Remove from heat and set aside. Put breadcrumbs in a food processor and blend until the crumbs are fine and soft. Pour breadcrumbs into a casserole dish and add Parmesan cheese. Mix well, then add the oyster mixture and blend well with the bread crumbs. Be sure the breadcrumbs are moist all the way through the casserole. If not, add more olive oil. Sprinkle 2 tbsp. Parmesan cheese on top and bake for 8 minutes. Turn the oven to broil and cook an additional 3 minutes. Check frequently. Remove from oven when browned. Squeeze the juice of ½ lemon over top of casserole. Serves 4.

Oyster and Crabmeat au Gratin

This luscious recipe comes to us from Kim Vandenborre of Slidell, Louisiana. "I like to cook; I just don't like to clean up the mess," she says as she flashes a one-thousand-megawatt smile. "I used to cook three meals a day. I had three children. Now I like to cook because I like to experiment—have special meals. I like it when someone says, 'Oh boy, that was good.'" My words exactly!

Watching Kim cook is fun. Husband Dudley is constantly meddling and supervising. Occasionally, she glances up and rolls her eyes. Dudley grins like a kid caught with his hand in a cookie jar. "I like to cook things different every time," he says. "I've messed up some dishes." Kim shakes her head in resignation.

Husband Dudley constantly meddles with Kim Vandenborre's cooking.

Tip: Kim prefers to use jumbo lump crabmeat because she likes to see the lumps, but less-expensive lump crabmeat works just as well.

Tip: This dish can be served as an entrée, appetizer, or as a sauce over fried fish.

1 stick butter, divided
½ cup chopped onion
¼ cup chopped celery
1 tbsp. minced garlic
1 cup chopped mushrooms
½ cup chopped green onions
4 tbsp. flour
3½ cups heavy whipping cream
Hot sauce to taste
1 tsp. lemon juice
1 cup grated mild cheddar cheese, divided
1½ tsp. Tony Chachere's Original Creole Seasoning
Granulated garlic, to taste
¼ cup parsley
1 pt. oysters, drained
1½ lb. jumbo lump crabmeat
Non-stick cooking spray

Preheat oven to 375 degrees. Melt ½ stick butter in a large saucepan. Add onion, celery, garlic, mushrooms, and green onions. Sauté until the vegetables are wilted. Add flour and stir to form a white roux. Pour in cream, lower heat, and whisk to make sure not to scorch. Cream should start to thicken to form a sauce. Simmer, adding hot sauce and lemon juice. Add ½ cup cheese and stir until melted. Season with Creole seasoning, granulated garlic, and parsley and cook an additional 7-10 minutes, stirring frequently. Set aside. In a separate pan, sauté oysters in ½ stick butter. Cook until all liquid evaporates. Spray a 2-qt. casserole dish with non-stick cooking spray. Add sauce, oysters, and crabmeat and stir gently to mix. Sprinkle remaining cheese on top. Bake 10-15 minutes until the cheese is melted. Serves 6.

Baked Oysters with Crab-Cream Sauce

New Orleans Creole cooking shows a heavy Italian influence. This dish is an example. The heavy hand of oysters doesn't overwhelm the crabmeat in this dish. They complement each other perfectly. Don't let the long list of ingredients scare you. Simply cut the ingredients up ahead of time and preparation will be quick.

1 pt. oysters, with liquor
¼ lb. butter
¼ cup diced onion
¼ cup diced celery
¼ cup diced red bell pepper
2 large cloves garlic, minced
¼ cup chopped green onion
½ lb. crabmeat
3 tbsp. flour
3 cups heavy whipping cream
1 jigger dry white wine
¾ cup sliced mushrooms
½ cup grated Parmesan cheese
1 jigger sherry
½ cup chopped parsley
2 egg yolks, beaten
Salt and cayenne pepper to taste
1 cup Italian breadcrumbs

Preheat oven to 450 degrees. Drain oysters, save the liquor, and set aside. In a 2-qt. heavy sauce pan, melt butter over medium-high heat. Add onion, celery, bell pepper, and garlic. Sauté approximately 3-5 minutes, until vegetables are wilted. Add green onion and crabmeat, blending well into vegetable mixture. Sprinkle in flour and whisk until smoothly mixed. The flour will act as a thickening agent for the sauce. Add heavy whipping cream and dry white wine. Stir constantly with wire whisk until the sauce begins to thicken. Add mushrooms and Parmesan cheese, stirring well as cheese melts and mixture continues to thicken. Add sherry and chopped parsley. If sauce is too thick, add oyster liquor. Remove pan from heat and quickly whisk in egg yolks.

Season to taste using salt and cayenne pepper. Allow to cool slightly or until sauce can be spooned without dripping. Spread the oysters in as shallow a layer as possible in a glass baking dish. Top with sauce and sprinkle the breadcrumbs over the mixture. Bake until sauce is bubbly and breadcrumbs are browned. Serve with good, hot bread. Serves 6.

Baked Oysters with Mushrooms

The mushrooms in this dish give it a nice, firm bite. If you feel experimental, crimini mushrooms will provide a more earthy, intense flavor than common Agaricus button mushrooms. Oysters are assertive enough to handle them. Lisa Winterburn, our friend and cooking and photographic assistant for the day, called this dish "great."

6 dozen medium oysters, with liquor
2 sticks butter, divided
1 cup chicken broth
2 small onions, chopped
4 cups chopped mushrooms
4 tbsp. flour
8 egg yolks, beaten
2 tbsp. lemon juice
½ tsp. minced parsley
Salt and pepper to taste
½ cup breadcrumbs

Tip: Add a little of the oyster liquor mixture to the egg yolks to warm them up before stirring the yolks into the mixture to prevent curdling.

Drain oysters and reserve liquor. Add oysters, 2 tbsp. butter, and chicken broth to saucepan. Cook until the edges of the oysters curl. Remove the oysters from liquid and set both aside. In another pot, sauté the onions and mushrooms in 6 tbsp. butter until soft. Stir in the flour and 4 tbsp. butter, and cook another 2 minutes. Add oyster liquor, and heat while stirring, until thick. Add oysters and egg yolks. Remove from heat and season with lemon juice, parsley, salt, and pepper. Put mixture in a buttered baking dish. Cover with breadcrumbs and dot with butter. Bake at 350 degrees until brown, 5-7 minutes. Serves 4.

Oysters Topped with Crabmeat

I first sampled this delightful dish when it was submitted by Soliska Cheramie of Lafourche Parish to a 4-H Seafood Cookery contest in 2001. I was lucky enough to be a judge. It was wonderful! Lump crabmeat is ideal for this dish, but claw meat will work too, as will jumbo lump meat if you want to spring for the cost of the latter.

2 dozen medium to large oysters with liquor
4 tbsp. butter
1 cup chopped green onions
4 sprigs parsley, chopped
4 tsp. flour
1 cup oyster liquor
1 lb. crabmeat
1 tsp. salt
½ tsp. red pepper
1 cup breadcrumbs

Drain oysters, save liquor, and set aside. Melt butter in a medium skillet. Add green onions and parsley and sauté until tender. Add flour and blend well. Add oyster liquor and stir briskly (If you don't have enough liquor to make a full cup, add water). Add crabmeat, salt, and pepper. Cook for two minutes, stirring constantly. Place oysters in a 9 x 13 inch baking dish. Pour crab mixture on top and sprinkle with breadcrumbs. Bake at 300 degrees for 25 minutes or until breadcrumbs are golden brown. Serves 4-6.

Tip: If oysters are unwashed or home-shucked, they may already be salty. If so, you may want to reduce the salt.

Scalloped Oyster Casserole

Scalloping by definition means to bake with milk or a sauce, often with breadcrumbs on top. It's not haute cuisine. There is nothing elaborate about this dish. It's just good—stick to the ribs good. Eat hearty!

1 stick butter
¼ cup chopped celery
1 small onion, chopped
1 tbsp. chopped parsley
1 tsp. salt
1 tsp. minced garlic
1 tsp. lemon juice
¼ tsp. black pepper
¼ tsp. hot sauce
1 pt. oysters with liquor
¾ cup half-and-half
2 cups, crushed cracker crumbs, divided
½ cup grated cheddar cheese

In a 2-qt. saucepan, combine butter, celery, onions, parsley, salt, garlic, lemon juice, pepper, and hot sauce. Sauté over medium heat until onions are soft. Add oysters with liquor and cook on high, stirring regularly until edges of oysters begin to curl. Add half-and-half and 1½ cups of cracker crumbs, and mix well. Spoon mixture into casserole dish; sprinkle cheddar cheese and rest of cracker crumbs on top. Bake in a 350 degree oven until cracker crumbs are golden in color. Serves 4.

Deviled Oysters

This recipe does not disguise the native taste of oysters, in spite of all the seasonings; instead, the ingredients showcase the oysters. This is another oyster dish that uses nutmeg, an ingredient many people today think of for use in baking sweets rather than in savory dishes. Historically, nutmeg has been a spice of choice in oyster cookery. If you like oysters, you will like this dish.

1½ pt. oysters, drained
2 tbsp. minced onion
4 tbsp. butter, divided
4 tbsp. flour
1½ cups milk
1 tsp. salt
¼ tsp. nutmeg
½ tsp. Tabasco sauce
1 tsp. prepared mustard
1 tbsp. Worcestershire sauce
1 tsp. chopped parsley
1 egg, beaten
½ cup breadcrumbs

Chop oysters and set aside. Cook onion in 2 tbsp. butter until tender. Blend in flour, add milk, and cook until thick, stirring constantly. Add salt, nutmeg, Tabasco sauce, mustard, Worcestershire sauce, parsley,

beaten egg, and oysters and heat. In a separate bowl, mix breadcrumbs with 2 tbsp. melted butter. Place oyster mixture in a glass baking dish and cover with buttered breadcrumbs. Bake in a 400 degree oven for 10 minutes, or until browned. Serves 4.

Tip: Whole nutmegs grated on a zester/grater or micro-plane add a much more heady taste and aroma than pre-grated nutmeg does.

Deviled Oyster Casserole

This dish has been in our recipe files since forever. It is a good one, but it's rich. I have never understood exactly what the word "deviled" meant. I got curious and did some research. It really seems that no one else knows either. Most commonly, reference was made to deviled foods being cooked in a hot or spicy way or with hot or spicy ingredients. Mustard seemed to meet their definition of spicy, which explained deviled eggs. But every deviled egg I ever ate was bland. Deviled ham doesn't have any mustard and really isn't hot either—it's just a good way to ruin perfectly good ham. Perhaps the best definition for "deviled" that I found was "What the Hell did you put in there?" It's vague, but it's humorous.

1 cup melted butter
1 cup finely diced onion
1 cup finely diced celery
½ cup finely diced red bell pepper
½ cup chopped green onions
1 tbsp. minced garlic
1 cup heavy whipping cream
2 pt. oysters in liquor
2 boiled eggs, diced
½ cup chopped parsley
1 tbsp. Worcestershire sauce
½ tsp. hot sauce
2½ cups seasoned Italian breadcrumbs
Salt to taste

Preheat oven to 350 degrees. In a 2-qt. saucepan, heat butter over medium-high heat. Sauté onion, celery, bell pepper, green onions, and garlic in the butter until wilted, approximately 2-3 minutes. Add heavy whipping cream, bring to a low boil, and reduce to simmer. Add oysters and oyster liquor and cook until oyster edges are slightly curled. Remove from heat and add egg, parsley, Worcestershire sauce, and hot sauce. Blend well into mixture. Sprinkle breadcrumbs, 1 cup at a time, until proper consistency is achieved. Mixture should remain moist but should hold together well with breadcrumbs. Salt to taste. Place in a well greased 9 x 13 inch baking pan or individual shells and bake for approximately 1 hour. Serves 6.

Oysters Rockefeller Casserole

This recipe, from Misty Faucheux of St. Charles Parish, came into our possession nineteen years ago. I loved it the first time I tried it and I still love it. I think that it is better than Oysters Rockefeller as served at Antoine's Restaurant, which is where the dish was invented. *The Antoine's Restaurant Cookbook* says that the recipe was created in 1899 when a shortage of snails, one of the restaurant's specialties, caused Jules Alciatore to shift his attention to oysters. The original recipe has never been released.

Although virtually everyone cooks their version of the dish today using spinach, Roy Guste, Jr., great grandson of Jules Alciatore, maintains that the sauce is basically a puree of a number of green vegetables other than spinach. Author and skeptic William Poundstone, in his 1989 book *Bigger Secrets*, reported that laboratory analysis of the dish indicated that the main ingredients were parsley, pureed and strained celery, scallions or chives, olive oil, and capers.

And the name? Jules Alciatore's September 13, 1934 obituary in the *New York Times* reported that in his own words he said that he named the dish "because I know of no other name rich enough for their richness."

2 sticks butter
1⅔ cups chopped green onions
1 cup chopped celery
1 large clove garlic, minced
1 tbsp. Worcestershire sauce
1½ cups seasoned breadcrumbs
4 dozen small oysters, drained, with liquor reserved
¾ cup chopped parsley
½ cup grated Parmesan cheese
3 10-oz. packages frozen, chopped spinach, cooked and drained
½ tsp. salt
¼ tsp. black pepper
¼ tsp. cayenne pepper

Melt the butter in a large skillet over moderate heat. Add green onions, celery, and garlic. Sauté for 5 minutes. Add the Worcestershire sauce and breadcrumbs and mix well. Cook until the breadcrumbs are toasted. Gently stir in oysters, ½ cup oyster liquor, parsley, Parmesan cheese, spinach, salt, black pepper, and cayenne pepper. Place in a 3-qt. casserole dish and bake at 375 degrees for 25 minutes. Serves 6.

Mad Madeleine

This is another of outdoor writer and TV host Joe Macaluso's camp cuisine recipes. "The recipe," he says, "is basically a Spinach Madeleine, but it isn't a Spinach Madeleine." Hmmm. Joe put the recipe together when the camp's usual cook, Bruce Scharwarth, had to go home. "The recipe evolved from spinach and cheese to spinach, cheese, and artichoke to spinach, cheese, artichoke, and oysters. It all depends on what you have at the camp." Our opinion: don't leave any of them out. It's good.

Joe and his wife Cheryl are a lot of fun in the kitchen. He is half-Italian, half-German by blood, but all Italian by heritage. Cheryl is, in her own words, "100 percent Cajun." Their marriage was culinary culture shock. "For the first two years," she says, "I wouldn't cook a red gravy. I didn't want him to tell me that it didn't taste as good as his family's."

Both love to cook; both love good food. Cheryl says that Joe sees it as fun and that she sees it as making it taste good—everything from scratch. Now, she says, their two sons, Joey and Chris, are both excellent cooks, with Chris being especially adventurous. "Here's what goes on at my table; they sit down and say it's really good. Then they start suggesting ways to change it."

Cheryl is especially proud of Joe's 2011 induction into the National Italian American Sports Hall of Fame. She informs everyone that she is now married to the "Top Wop."

Joe Macaluso frets about bringing camp cooking home for wife Cheryl to try.

Tip: Joe recommends not using expensive imported cheeses, because they are too hard and add a grainy surface texture to the dish. Besides, you would never find the imported stuff at a hunting camp anyway, so using it wouldn't be authentic.

Tip: Joe says that if you double the recipe, do not increase the amount of sour cream.

3 10-oz. packages frozen chopped spinach
½ cup finely chopped onion
1 stick unsalted butter
½ tsp. red pepper
3 dozen oysters
1 pt. sour cream
⅓ cup Parmesan cheese
½ tsp. sea salt
1 14-oz. can artichoke hearts, coarsely chopped
½ cup Romano/Parmesan cheese blend
1 tsp. chopped parsley

Preheat oven to 350 degrees. Cook spinach according to package directions. Drain well and set aside. Sauté onion in butter until tender. The edges should begin to toast to add color to the dish. Add red pepper and oysters. Simmer until the edges of the oysters curl, gently stirring to prevent sticking. Turn off heat and let cool. Add sour cream to spinach, and mix well. Add Parmesan cheese and sea salt. Fold in artichoke hearts. Add the oyster mixture to the spinach and mix well. Spoon into a casserole dish and sprinkle with Parmesan/Romano cheese blend and parsley. Bake for 30 minutes.

Oysters Bienville

Oysters Bienville is an old New Orleans dish with a disputed pedigree. Some would attribute its invention to Pete Michel and Roy Alciatore of Antoine's Restaurant. Others credit "Count" Arnaud Cazeneuve at Arnaud's with its creation. And then some split the difference, claiming that Cazeneuve recreated the dish, which he first tasted at Antoine's. Claims for the date of invention range from the late 1930s to the early 1940s. Food history, like genealogy, can be tedious. The dish is named for Jean Baptiste Le Moyne, Sieur de Bienville, governor of French Louisiana and father of New Orleans, Louisiana; Biloxi, Mississippi; and Mobile, Alabama.

4 dozen oysters on the half-shell
2 lb. cooked shrimp
2 6.5-oz. cans mushrooms
5 cloves garlic
1 large onion
1½ cups milk
1½ cups chicken broth
1 cup butter
½ cup cream
¼ cup sherry
4 tbsp. flour
Salt and pepper to taste
1 4-lb. box rock salt
¼ lb. thin-sliced bacon, fried crisply and crumbled
¼ cup chopped green onions
1 lb. grated sharp cheddar cheese
Seasoned breadcrumbs
1 tsp. smoked paprika

Drain any excess liquid off the oysters and set them aside. Chop the shrimp, mushrooms, garlic, and onion in a food processor. In a medium saucepan, mix the milk, broth, butter, cream, sherry, and flour. Add chopped ingredients and salt and pepper, and simmer slowly for 15 minutes. Put drained oysters in their shells on a bed of rock salt in a baking pan and broil for 2 minutes. Remove from oven

Tip: Cooking this dish on a bed of rock salt is traditional. Not only does the salt stabilize the oyster shells for cooking, it retains heat well.

Tip: White wine is an acceptable, if not exact, substitute for sherry.

and drain liquid from oysters. Spoon sauce over each oyster and broil an additional 2 minutes. Remove from the oven and sprinkle with bacon, green onions, cheese, breadcrumbs, and paprika. Return to broiler and brown. Serve hot. Serves 4-6.

Smoked Pork and Oyster Jambalaya

I am especially proud of my brown chicken and sausage jambalaya, so it was only natural that I began to experiment with seafood in it. This one works really well. The only hitch is that you will need smoked pork. We cook pork shoulders and butts on a wood smoker frequently, so we have a lot of leftover pork on hand.

I know that to some people, my use of Minute Rice is heresy. I fought the liquid to rice ratio for years. Most of the time I managed to hit it right, but more times than I care to admit, I had a tad too much rice for the liquid and it didn't completely soften or I had too much liquid and the rice became mushy.

An old jambalaya hand, Roland "Boudreaux" Trahan, came to our family hunting camp in the Atchafalaya Basin and turned me on to using Minute Rice in jambalayas. Then I cooked Minute Rice jambalaya at another hunting camp in Ascension Parish, where the World Jambalaya Cook-off is held. It met rave reviews and I never looked back. As much as I swear by instant rice for jambalaya, though, I never use it for anything else.

2 lb. smoked pork
1 pt. oysters, with liquor
⅓ cup cooking oil
3 cups chopped onions
¾ cup chopped bell pepper
¾ cup chopped celery
5 cloves garlic, minced
3 tbsp. brown roux
4 bay leaves
2½ tsp. salt
1½ tsp. pepper
¼ cup chopped parsley
¾ cup chopped green onion
1 28-oz. box Minute Rice

Cut smoked pork into 1-inch cubes. Drain the oysters and save the liquor. Pour oil into a large pot, preferably cast iron. Add onions, bell pepper, celery, and garlic and sauté over medium-low heat until seasonings are clear and have lightly toasted edges. Add enough water to the oyster liquor to make 2 qt. and add to seasonings. Add roux, turn heat to high, and bring to a boil to dissolve the roux. Add bay leaves and pork. Cover tightly and bring to a boil. Reduce heat and simmer ½ hour. Add salt, pepper, oysters, and parsley. Cover and simmer 10 minutes, until oysters are done. Add green onions and simmer 5 more minutes. Reduce heat to low. Add Minute Rice and stir well. Allow dish to sit, covered, for 10 minutes. Uncover and check the rice. If the rice is soft, but unabsorbed liquid remains, stir in a little more rice. If no liquid remains, but rice is still a little hard, add ¼ cup of water at a time, stirring gently after each addition, until the rice is soft and no liquid is present. Serves 6-8.

Lois' Seafood Jambalaya

Tip: The rice can be cooked a day ahead to save time while cooking.

Tip: This amount of oysters is more a seasoning than a main ingredient. If you really like oysters, you may want to double the amount of oysters.

When you hear the word jambalaya, you just naturally think of Louisiana. And seafood jambalaya is the best jambalaya there is. I was lucky enough to get Lois Robeaux of Lafitte to share her recipe with us. This is a most unusual jambalaya in that the rice is cooked ahead in plain water and then later mixed with the other ingredients, rather than being cooked in the savory broth of the other ingredients. This jambalaya is "New Orleans Creole-style," meaning it is a red, tomato jambalaya, rather than a brown, Cajun jambalaya.

3 cups rice
1 large onion, chopped
⅔ cup chopped shallots
⅔ cup chopped bell pepper
⅔ cup chopped parsley
⅔ cup cooking oil
3 lb. medium shrimp, peeled
1 8-oz. can tomato sauce
1 lb. smoked sausage, cut in slices
3 cups water
1 dozen oysters
1 lb. crabmeat
2 tsp. salt
1 tsp. black pepper

Boil rice and set aside. Sauté onion, shallots, bell pepper, and parsley over medium-low heat in cooking oil until tender. Add shrimp and cook 10 minutes, stirring occasionally. Stir in tomato sauce and cook 5 more minutes, stirring repeatedly. Add smoked sausage and cook 10 additional minutes. Pour in 3 cups of water and cook for 30 minutes over medium heat. Add oysters and crabmeat and cook 15 minutes. Salt and pepper to taste. Add rice a little at a time, steadily stirring, until all the rice is used. Cook over medium heat for 15 minutes, stirring occasionally. Serves 6-8.

Rita LaCava's Erster (Oyster) Dressing

We were never big fans of that great Louisiana holiday tradition—oyster dressing—until Charlie Smith of Baton Rouge, Louisiana, converted us. He brought a container of this leftover dressing to my duck hunting camp after Christmas, years ago. It never made it to the stove. The hunters ate the entire tub cold, arguing over the last morsel. It is superb! Charlie says that this is his late mother-in-law Rita LaCava's recipe, with only one addition of his own: fennel water. Rita and her husband, Salvador, Isleños from Delacroix Island who lived through the great Mississippi River flood of 1927, had their home wiped out when Hurricane Katrina flooded St. Bernard Parish. Charlie is the executive director of the Louisiana Charter Boat Association and a lobbyist in the Louisiana Legislature, as well as being an excellent cook, superb raconteur, enthusiastic waterfowl hunter and fisherman, and the state's most outspoken defender of fine arts; in sum he is a character with character.

For this recipe, Charlie insists that oyster liquor (water from oysters as they are shucked into a container) is necessary. Commercially packed oysters are typically thoroughly washed and packed in tap water, which Charlie insists (and we agree) is not the same. Go to any lengths to find such oysters in their own liquor, or buy a half-gallon of oyster liquor separately from a shucking house. Shucking our own oysters is our preference.

This is the style of coarse bread crumbs needed for this dish.

Tip: This can be a good dish for holiday cooking, because all preparation is done the day before it is cooked.

Tip: If you can't find Riesing's breadcrumbs, very slowly dry out 2½ loaves of French bread in a very low heat oven and crumble it. Do not use dried Progresso-type breadcrumbs, because they are far too small to produce proper consistency.

1 gal. oysters, with liquor
1 gal. additional oyster liquor
1 tsp. fennel seeds
1 cup water
Cooking oil
4 medium to large onions, chopped
2 bunches green onions, chopped
1 stalk celery, chopped
5 cloves garlic, minced
½ bunch parsley, chopped
2 18-oz. bags Riesing breadcrumbs
Tony Chachere's Original Creole Seasoning to taste

Drain the oysters and save the liquor. Reserve 6-8 attractive oysters to put on top of the casserole before baking. Chop the rest of the oysters finely in a food processor. Put the fennel seeds in 1 cup water, bring to a boil, and simmer for 15-20 minutes. Strain oyster liquor and set aside. Pour oil in a large pot; add onions, green onions, celery, and garlic; and sauté until soft over medium heat. Add parsley, fennel water, and half of the oyster liquor. Add the breadcrumbs and mix well. Add chopped oysters and mix well. Add more liquor if needed to keep the mixture moist. Cover and continue to cook for about 30 minutes, stirring and adding more liquor or oil as needed to keep a thick, but pliable, consistency. Turn heat off and cool enough to refrigerate overnight. Bake in a baking dish in a 350 degree oven for 45-60 minutes. Serves 12 as a side dish for holiday dinner.

Oyster-Rice Dressing

Rose Palombo cooks every day for family, but she calls cooking her therapy.

Tip: If you can't find Guidry's Creole Seasoning mix in the fresh produce aisle, you can make your own using 2¼ cups chopped onions, ½ cup chopped bell pepper, ½ cup chopped celery, ½ cup chopped green onions, ¼ cup chopped parsley, and 5 cloves minced garlic.

Tip: The meat and oyster mixture can be divided and part used in a rice dressing and the other part in a cornbread dressing. Just add crumbled cornbread instead of rice.

In the heart of Cajun Country, when you say dressing, you mean rice dressing, a tony name for dirty rice. "When you see a Cajun, you see the rice following him," says Rose Palombo of Lafayette, whose recipe this is. "We ate rice every day. Mom used to eat it with butter and milk. That was our menu back then. When we didn't have rice, we would have cornbread or couche couche. They went far.

"I'm pure Cajun. My mom was a Simon (pronounced SEE-moan) and my dad was a Hebert (pronounced A-bear)." Rose's Italian surname comes from her husband Kenneth, who is part Italian and part Cajun. "Cooking is my therapy. It keeps me sane," says Rose. "I really wanted to be a chef, but I think that God had something else in mind. This recipe is my mother's that I changed some things on."

5 cups medium grain rice
4 tbsp. cooking oil
4 cups Guidry's Creole Seasoning mix
1 cup Pat's Old Fashioned Iron Pot Roux
4 cups water
3 tbsp. Tony Chachere's Original Creole Seasoning
1 tbsp. salt
5 lb. chicken gizzards, chopped
3 lb. lean ground chuck
1 qt. oysters
3 green onions, finely chopped

Cook rice and set aside. Put oil and Guidry's Creole Seasoning mix in a large pot and sauté over medium heat until light brown. Add the roux and water, stirring until the roux dissolves, making a gravy. Add Tony Chachere's Creole Seasoning and salt, and simmer 45 minutes. Stir in the chopped gizzards and add crumbled ground chuck. Cook an additional 45 minutes, stirring occasionally. Add oysters and simmer 10 minutes. Sprinkle in the green onions. Put cooked rice in a large bowl and add the meat and oyster mixture a little at a time until you get the desired moistness to the dressing. Any left-over mixture can be put on the table for those who like their dressing moister. Serves 15-20 at a holiday dinner.

Oyster-Water Chestnut Stuffing

Three types of stuffing are traditionally cooked in Louisiana. Cornbread stuffings are more common in north Louisiana, breadcrumb stuffings prevail in the New Orleans area, and rice stuffings are a Cajun tradition. This one is a cornbread stuffing that has been jazzed up with water chestnuts. Their delightful crunch adds a whole 'nother dimension to the dish. The sage is a nice touch too.

1 pt. oysters, with liquor
1 cup finely chopped onion
½ cup chopped celery
¼ cup chopped parsley
½ cup butter
1 8-oz. pkg. cornbread stuffing mix
1 egg, beaten
1 8-oz. can sliced water chestnuts, drained
1 tsp. salt
½ tsp. thyme
½ tsp. sage
¼ tsp. black pepper

Drain oysters and reserve liquor. Sauté onion, celery, and parsley in butter until tender. Do not brown. Add enough water to reserved oyster liquor to make 1 cup. In a bowl, combine stuffing mix, egg, and liquor and mix lightly to blend. Stir in sautéed vegetables, water chestnuts, and seasonings. Spoon the stuffing loosely into the cavity of a 10 to 12 pound turkey. If the stuffing is to be baked separately from turkey, bake at 350 degrees for 15-20 minutes. Serves 6.

Rice is Nice

No single food item is so essential to South Louisiana cuisine as rice. It is the starch of choice for both the "prairie Cajuns" west of the Atchafalaya Basin and the "bayou Cajuns" of the eastern half of the state. Although rice is rivaled in popularity by pasta in New Orleans Creole cuisine, rice is still dominant for Cajuns.

Cajun stews, beans, and both onion and brown gravies are commonly served over rice. Rice is so beloved among Cajuns that it is often eaten and relished unadorned by anything but melted butter. Rice is also frequently eaten topped only with canned, cream-style corn. Soft-fried eggs broken over rice serve as Cajun comfort food. Glenda's father, "Nappy Ray," was so addicted to rice and gravy or rice and beans that anything and everything else was relegated to the inferior category of "dry food."

With their current love affair with rice, it is hard to believe that Cajuns didn't always eat rice as their staple grain. But rice certainly wasn't in their diet in Nova Scotia. The cold Canadian climate wasn't suitable for rice, so wheat and barley were their staple grains.

After the Acadian diaspora of 1755, the exiles that came to South Louisiana found the climate unfriendly to the cultivation of wheat and barley, so they grew corn as a staple grain. Travelers repeatedly noted the dominance of corn in the Cajun diet from 1786 through most of the 1800s. Rice was indeed planted in the Cajun heartland, but it was a marginal crop that depended on unpredictable spring rains to flood the fields for successful growth.

After 1850, until the end of the Civil War, significant commercial rice production did occur in Louisiana along the Mississippi River, on the extreme eastern margin of Cajun country. The river served as a dependable irrigation source, because its waters could be pumped over the river levees into the rice fields.

With the abolition of slavery, U.S. rice production, both in South Carolina—where it began in the U.S. in 1685—and in Louisiana, declined severely. South Carolina's rice industry completely disappeared. Two factors sparked the survival and development of rice farming in Louisiana.

First was the introduction of steam power for milling rice in the mid-1880s. Second, in 1884, an Iowa wheat farmer discovered that the firm prairie soils of southwestern Louisiana and southeastern Texas could support the use of heavy machinery to farm rice, much like wheat is farmed. Mechanized rice farming was rapidly adopted, both

The world's rice varieties come in many shapes and almost every color of the rainbow.

by Louisianians and immigrant Midwestern farmers, who moved to the area to farm rice. By the 1920s, rice consumption had caught on well amongst Cajuns.

Rice is a staple grain for nearly half of the people on earth, although 95 percent of it is grown and eaten in Asia. In some countries, rice is eaten three times a day and consumption approaches four hundred pounds per person.

About twenty species of rice exist, only two of which are domesticated: Asian rice, *Oryza sativa*, and African rice, *Oryza glaberrima*. Asian rice so completely dominates the world's rice production that it has largely replaced African rice in Africa.

Rice is generally classified by the shape of the grain. Long-grain rice has a long and slender kernel and is very high in amylose starch. When cooked, the grains remain separate and fluffy and are somewhat dry. This is the dominant rice grown and eaten in Louisiana. It may be referred to as indica rice.

Medium-grain rice is shorter and plumper and has a lower amylose content. It cooks up stickier and moister than long-grain rice. Short-grain rice (japonica) has a shorter and rounder kernel yet and is very sticky and moist. The final classification, glutinous rice, has the lowest amylose content and is extremely sticky. This is the rice used in sushi and rice balls.

Most rice varieties are sold as either white or brown rice. They are the same grain, but brown rice does not have the bran around the kernel milled off. Brown rice also takes about twice as long to cook as does white rice. It is more nutritious and has a firmer bite. Brown rice has a much shorter shelf life than white rice and should be refrigerated if it will be kept more than three months. White rice can be kept almost indefinitely in a sealed container.

White rice is more tender and delicate than brown rice and may be purchased enriched to restore some nutrients. Converted rice, which is tan in color, also has more nutrients and tastes very similar to white rice. Converted rice is steamed before it is husked, causing the grains to absorb nutrients from the husk. Instant rice is simply rice that has been precooked and dried.

In recent years, basmati and various aromatic rice varieties are finding favor in Louisiana kitchens. Basmati is a long-grain rice that has been cultivated near the Himalayan foothills for centuries. It is especially popular in India and Pakistan. It has a nutty flavor and is very aromatic. The name literally interprets as "queen of fragrance."

Like basmati rice, aromatic rices fill the kitchen with delightful "roasted nut" aromas while being cooked. Louisiana wild pecan rice, popcorn rice, and Texmati rice are all aromatic rice. Della rice is a hybrid between basmati and American long-grain rice. It has a shorter grain than basmati, but it is considered an aromatic variety.

Thai jasmine rice is a long-grain aromatic rice with a subtle floral aroma. It originated in Thailand. Jasmati rice is a registered trademarked brand of jasmine rice grown in the United States.

Oyster Pizza

Oysters work well with pizza, especially one like this with lots of olives, peppers, and onions. Less assertive seafood, such as shrimp, does not have enough presence and tends to disappear into the background flavor of the dish. 'Course that's only my opinion. Glenda prefers the dish with shrimp.

Sauce

1 8-oz. can tomato sauce
1 6-oz. can tomato paste
1 tbsp. chopped parsley
1 tbsp. Italian seasoning
½ tsp. minced basil
½ tsp. sugar
¼ cup dry red wine

Mix all of the sauce ingredients together in a saucepan. Cover and simmer for 10 minutes.

Pizza

1 loaf frozen Bridgeford bread dough
4 cups grated mozzarella cheese, divided
½ cup thinly slivered bell pepper
½ cup thinly slivered onion
½ cup sliced black olives
¼ cup sliced green olives, optional
1 4-oz. can mushrooms
1 pt. oysters

Place the frozen bread dough in a warm place in the kitchen and allow it to thaw and rise for 6-8 hours. Roll out the dough on a floured surface. Spread dough in a 10 x 15-inch greased, glass baking dish. Spread the sauce evenly over the dough. Sprinkle 1 cup mozzarella cheese evenly over the sauce. Arrange the bell peppers, onion, olives, mushrooms, and oysters over the entire pizza. Top with 3 cups mozzarella cheese. Bake in pre-heated 400 degree oven for 20 minutes, or until crust is lightly brown. Serves 4.

Deep Dish Oyster Pie

We have shared this recipe with many friends, and they never fail to enjoy it. It was presented to me in 1982 by the late Margaret Barron, a home economist with the Louisiana Cooperative Extension Service. Margaret, a charmer and a good cook, began her LSU career in 1948. This was one of her favorite personal recipes. It is moist and not aggressively seasoned. Although it has much more celery than onions, unusual for a Louisiana dish, it is not at all unbalanced.

1 pt. oysters, with liquor
4 tbsp. butter
2 tbsp. minced onions
½ cup diced celery
3 tbsp. flour
Milk as needed
Salt to taste
Freshly ground pepper
Dash Tabasco sauce
1 pastry crust

Drain oysters and save liquor. In a large saucepan, melt the butter. Add onion and celery and sauté until soft, about 5 minutes. Stir in flour and cook for 2 minutes. Add enough milk to reserved oyster liquor to make 2 cups. Add liquid to pan and cook, stirring constantly until thickened and smooth. Add oysters and cook until edges curl. Season with salt, pepper, and Tabasco sauce. Pour mixture into a greased 1-qt. baking dish and cool. Preheat oven to 400 degrees. Put pastry crust on top of casserole and seal the edges. Bake for 25 to 30 minutes, until the crust is golden. Makes 4 generous servings.

Spicy Oyster Pie

A good oyster pie is hard to beat. It is a traditional Louisiana dish, especially in New Orleans. But the dish is never on restaurant menus, probably because it is difficult to produce an attractive presentation once the pie crust has been broken. Most pies made in the United States today are sweet pies, often filled with fruit. But pies originally were savory. The first pies were made by early Romans and were seafood or meat-filled. In medieval Merrie Olde England, pies were still primarily meat-filled, although some were spiced with fruit. These are the pies that the Pilgrims brought to America. Gradually, through the eighteen, nineteenth, and twentieth centuries sweet pies dominated the pie scene. This spicy recipe is excellent. I love it.

1 pt. oysters, with liquor
½ cup flour
¾ cup milk
2 stalks celery, chopped
1 clove garlic, minced
½ cup chopped bell pepper
¼ cup chopped parsley
1 tsp. black pepper
1 tsp. red pepper
1 tsp. salt
2 9-in. pie shells

Drain oysters and reserve liquor. Brown flour in a cast-iron skillet until it darkens (Note: no oil is added to flour). Add milk and stir well. Add oysters to skillet. Cook 15 minutes or until oysters become firm. If mixture is too thick, add oyster liquor. Add chopped ingredients and seasonings. Add salt last to prevent curdling the milk. Place oyster mixture in unbaked pie shell and cover with top crust. Start pie at 450 degrees and cook for 15 minutes. Reduce heat to 350 degrees and continue cooking until brown. Serves 4.

Index